DATE DUE		

D0028270

Trail Safe

Averting Threatening
Human Behavior in the Outdoors

Michael Bane

WILDERNESS PRESS
BERKELEY

APPALACHIAN TRAIL CONFERENCE
HARPERS FERRY, WEST VIRGINIA

Published by: **Wilderness Press**
1200 5th Street
Berkeley, CA 94710
(800) 443-7227 • Fax (510) 558-1696
mail@wildernesspress.com

Visit our website www.wildernesspress.com
Contact us for a free catalog

  Printed on recycled paper, 20% post-consumer waste

Library of Congress Cataloging-in-Publication Data

Bane, Michael, 1950-
    Trail Safe: averting threatening human behavior in the outdoors /
    Michael Bane.-- 1st ed. p. cm.
    Includes index.
    ISBN 0-89997-264-0 (alk. paper)
    1. Outdoor recreation--Safety measures. 2. Wilderness survival. 3. Risk-
    taking (Psychology) I. Title

GV 191.625 .B25 2000   00-023562

Dedication

To my father and to Jayne, who saved his life.
And to Denise, as always.

Contents

Acknowledgments

A variety of people assisted me throughout the conceptualization and the execution of this book, and they all deserve my recognition and gratitude. First, I thank the Appalachian Trail Conference for their hand in co-publishing this book and for their continuing belief in and contributions to the project. I thank Michael Hodgson, who referred me to Wilderness Press when asked for his recommendation of someone who had the experience necessary to write a book on personal safety in the wilderness. Also, I extend kudos to my editor at Wilderness Press, Robin White, for her good work.

In addition to the people mentioned above, I would like to thank Walt Rauch, Massad Ayoob, Dane Burns, John Shaw, and John Orlowski for the immense impact each has had on my life. Lastly, thank you to all of the friends who have crossed paths with me, whether on the trail or elsewhere.

Michael Bane
February 2000

1

Introduction

A Walk in the Woods

AH, THE BACKCOUNTRY. The woods, the forest, the hills, the mountains, the pristine air—all the elements of nature converge to create our concept of the outdoors. We have extracted joy from the outdoors throughout history, and its endless beauty has inspired music, literature, philosophy, and poetry in every era. Despite humanity's historical love of the outdoors, the backcountry has another side to it, a menacing side. I had occasion not too long ago to engage in some research on the Middle Ages. During my studies, I was struck by the way in which our medieval ancestors viewed the dark woods. Overwhelmingly, the places we think of today as the backcountry were viewed as haunts of evil, home to all manner of man-eating beasts (real and imagined), as well as to men who were themselves little better than beasts. A walk in the woods inspired fear, a dread that death—or perhaps something worse—waited just around the next tree. Think about this medieval nursery rhyme:

> *"Who's afraid of the big, bad wolf,*
> *The big, bad wolf,*
> *The big, bad wolf?"*

We have come a long, long way from that apprehensive wariness of the backcountry. These strong historical beliefs contrast mightily with our current view of the outdoors as a respite from urban life and a spring that rejuvenates both body and spirit.

As we begin a new millennium, I sense a little of that medieval fear creeping back into the dark woods. This time, the fear is generated not by the big, bad wolf or by other assorted creatures of nightmare or legend. Instead, it originates from the creatures that populate our new nightmares and latest urban legends: our fellow human beings who choose us as prey. It is indeed an irony that, for those of us who fled urban America for the safe and peaceful solitude of trails, back roads, and wild places, we wound up bringing along with us the very things we fled.

I believe, however, that the most fearsome things we now bring with us to the wild places are not our predators themselves, but the fear of the predators, the fear of the unknown. That thought was brought home to me after the 1999 murders of three women near California's Yosemite National Park. Following the murders, the media focused heavily on stories about the rise of crime in the backcountry. Some stories were true and informative, while others, though true, left out some facts. For example, though the murdered women were kidnapped just outside a national park, they were kidnapped from their hotel room, not from a campsite. Such details lead to misconceptions by the public about what is actually occurring and what they should be prepared for.

Is the number of crimes in the backcountry on the increase?

Absolutely. A simple equation you'll see over and over again in *Trail Safe*, prey attracts predators. I have traveled extensively both in the backcountry and in dicey places in the Third World, and I have never seen those words disproved. *Prey attracts predators.* Thus, because of the sheer number of outdoor enthusiasts now entering the backcountry, the predators have picked up on the scent and trail close behind. And it has been my observation that, among prey, it is the weakest—the least prepared—that are the most at risk.

But is there a crime wave going on in the backcountry?

Absolutely not. As an illustration, take the Appalachian Trail along the eastern spine of America. Three to four million hikers per year walk portions of the Trail, yet just nine murders have occurred in 22 years. That's about a week's worth of murders in any large urban area. The aforementioned murders of the women (and of a subsequently discovered fourth victim) near Yosemite made national headlines precisely because they happened near a famous national park. However, they actually were not backcountry crimes.

Why *Trail Safe?*

I wrote this book because I believe that perceptions that lead to fear of a crime are as dangerous as, or perhaps ultimately more dangerous than, the crime itself. The fear of the dark woods poisons what, to me, can be one of the most rewarding things in life—spending time away from the crowds in nature's splendor.

I have been lucky enough to have, as they say, a "checkered" career. During the last decade or so, I've been an active participant in high-risk sports, and have supplemented that participation with extensive magazine and book writing featuring these sports as topics. My activities have included (but are not limited to) mountaineering, cave diving, and ultraendurance events such as the run across Death Valley and the snowshoe race on Alaska's Iditarod Trail.

I am decidedly non-athletic; in high school, I was always the kid who was picked last, no matter the sport. In the 1980s, however, I began studying the martial arts and eventually earned a black belt in Tang Soo Do, a Korean form of defense similar to Tae Kwan Do. I studied other arts, including Aikido, Kali/Escrima and T'ai Chi. I have also been a competitive target shooter for years.

Through my connection with martial arts and shooting, I found myself working with police agencies on their instructional programs for new officers. Police firearms training was going through an upheaval at the time, and instructors were looking outside traditional police circles for help. They found me. I trained with police SWAT teams to help discover flaws in their training; I became an expert at "killing" cops, working in controlled simulations as a guest bad guy; I spent a week being trained by the military to think like a terrorist, to become an even better bad guy.

At the same time, I was training with some of the finest competitive shooters in the world and exploring a series of esoteric activities, from spending time with a mime to learn how other people move to studying neuro-linguistic programming, a field within the realm of psychology.

My checkered background came together when I discovered that there existed a huge amount of information about how people performed at critical stress levels, but that this information was compartmentalized. Police had a bit; the military had a lot; rock climbers and mountaineers had a piece; cave divers had learned their own lessons. But the level of exchange of this information was amazingly low. I began synthesizing all of these pieces of information after I headed out into the wild. I watched how I performed under critical stress, and made changes as I went along. This synthesis and experimentation resulted in the following Six Rules for Planning Outrageous Trips, which we'll discuss a little later in the book at greater length:

- Choose a Summit
- Abandon your Comfort Zone
- Understand the Risks
- Narrow your Focus
- When in Doubt, Go Faster
- Embrace Chaos

These Six Rules have helped me up the slopes of Alaska's Mt. McKinley (20,320 feet) and Mexico's Pico de Orizaba (18,701 feet). They've helped me dive to more than 250 feet while breathing strange gases, explore the flooded caves of the Yucatan and north Florida, race mountain bikes downhill at speeds greater than 60 miles per hour, and raft and kayak some of the great Class V white-water rivers of the world.

More importantly, the Six Rules led me to an understanding of a different way to live. I'll be talking about the concept of living strategically and living purposefully in the moment. Heaven knows you've all heard, read, or been told that living in the moment is a worthy goal to seek. I want to provide you now with a set of tools to help you get there. Living strategically is also a way of living more safely. The world is a more dangerous place than it was five years ago. I want you to understand that you already have the tools to adapt to a less-safe world. All you need to do is learn to use them.

I treasure the moments I've spent in the backcountry, whether on foot, on snowshoes, on a mountain bike, in mountaineering boots or whatever. I also treasure what I've inherited from those moments: a level of self-reliance that has changed my life. The lessons I've learned have led me to working in ways I never dreamed of. For instance, I spend a lot of time these days talking to corporate executives about understanding and facilitating change, and most of the lessons I teach them I myself have learned in the outdoors.

The *Trail Safe* Tools

One of the things that fascinated me about the cultures associated with high-risk sports—and they are, indeed, distinct cultures—is how they deal with fear. The more time I spent doing activities that could kill me, the more I came to understand that fear, in its purest form, was a superb tool, a magnificent piece of "software" designed to help me stay alive under the most extreme circumstances. Yet we ourselves often compromise this great tool, rendering it worthless.

Trail Safe is designed to help you understand what fear is, and what it is not. It's designed to allow you to use fear and the other tools you already possess to banish false fear, that overwhelming sense of dread that keeps us from accomplishing the things we desire. *Trail Safe* is based upon my own belief that the way to banish false fears is by shining a light on them, to pick them up and examine them in the cold light of day. In that light, we find out where the real risks lie, and what we must do to overcome them.

When I first started ice climbing (climbing frozen waterfalls) I would lie wide-awake in bed the night before the climb while nameless fears crawled through my head. Even now, I continue to suffer from a fear of heights; looking over the edge of a cliff will give me a solid, piercing message of fear. The frozen waterfalls drew me to them, yet they profoundly scared me. The challenge ultimately became not how to climb ice, but how to deal with the fear that climbing ice seemed to generate in my head.

Strangely enough, I found my first hints of an answer in an old novel, *Dune*, by Frank Herbert. In that science-fiction epic, a sect of female witches habitually chanted a litany against fear that went something like this: "I will not fear . . . fear is the mind-killer . . . fear is the little death that brings the total oblivion." These wise women believed that fear numbed the mind and prohibited action. But fear is not something to be conquered; rather, it is more of a natural force, something to be allowed to flow over you, around you, and through you. Fear is a message.

The idea of overcoming fear, of conquering fear summons feelings of great seduction. But fear is never conquered, never overcome. You can bury it deeply until you think you've prevailed, only to have it pop up at the worst possible time. Or you can deal with, face it, as *Dune*'s litany suggests, and let it flow over you, around you, through you. Then, like a storm, it will pass.

Trail Safe provides tools for examining the dangers, both real and imagined, that we face when we choose to leave the protective confines of our urban environment. I'm not a self-defense guru, nor do I have any secret mystical wisdom from far places to impart. Rather, I want to show you a way to think about things you do not necessarily want to think about. I believe that this way of thinking has saved my life on more than one occasion.

I can tell you in advance that we will visit some places in *Trail Safe* that aren't very pleasant. We're going to look at some cherished beliefs, and they aren't going to hold up under close examination. We're going to have to ask ourselves some questions that, realistically, we'd rather avoid.

But the results are worth it.

A Map to *Trail Safe*

We're first going to participate in some exercises to help us see the world as it really exists, rather than as we've come to believe it might exist. Then we're going to examine in some detail our three-pronged self-defense mechanism, comprising *intuition, awareness, and fear.* How are the three linked? In what ways do they work together? How might we learn to take advantage of these powerful tools? Next we're going to study how we can prepare for a backcountry excursion in advance, both by assessing risks and by engaging in some basic planning. Finally, we're going to dive into the murky waters of how to deal with an actual violent encounter, taking it step-by-step from your mindset at the beginning to the conclusion of the encounter itself.

I'm making some basic assumptions up front, the largest of which is that you're reasonably experienced in the outdoors. You already know to let someone know where you're going and what your expected return date and time are. You already know that traveling alone carries with it heightened risks. You understand what carrying fundamental survival gear (knife, waterproof matches, a little food, filter or iodine tablets, duct tape, and so on) entails. *Trail Safe* is the next step along the line; it will give you psychological and reactionary tools that will keep you safe from emerging threats.

The last time I thought about "The Big, Bad Wolf" nursery rhyme was in Alaska last winter when, in the middle of the night, a wolf pack began to trail me. I think I even sang the ditty aloud, sitting on my sled full of survival gear, to the edification of Br'er Wolf. I was tired, sore, cold and, generally, in relatively bad humor, but I wasn't afraid of becoming wolf-chow because of the very tools outlined in *Trail Safe*.

The tools work, and they work against predators more fearful than wolves.

2

The Real World

Reality-Based Living

I WISH IT WEREN'T SO, but when you travel as much as I do, you end up watching a lot of bad television. Say what you will about reading great books or surfing the Internet. Sooner or later, it's 3 A.M. and you're watching "Our Friend the Dung Beetle" on the all-insect-all-the-time channel. A few months ago, I actually stumbled onto something on one of these channels that interested me: a story of the legendary killer bees. Killer bees, as you may know, are African honeybees that began colonizing the Americas in the 1950s and have a tendency to swarm readily when disturbed.

After presenting several images of killer bees swarming over farm animals and farmhands in the United States, the program cut to Tanzania, the bees' country of origin, where local tribesmen were harvesting honey from cultivated killer-bee hives. They did this at night by first puffing a little smoke inside and then sticking their bare hands into the hives and pulling out the honeycombs. The tribesmen have been doing this for generations, and since they didn't know that their bees were "killer bees," they didn't feel the need to run and hide, or to perhaps make a Tanzanian Movie of the Week dealing with the bees' savage tempers.

Let's talk about reality.

Which reality is more accurate: a panicked homeowner in Texas trying to fend off a phalanx of dive-bombing bees or Tanzanian tribesmen licking the honey off their fingers?

Our reality, or their reality?

In fact, I believe that both of these realities are accurate. The Tanzanian beekeepers have been gathering honey for generations, have cultivated the bees, and have developed immunity to the stings. Conversely, many people in the United States worry about the bees' ability to swarm and inflict enough stings to be potentially deadly. Bees sting; it's part of what they do. Actually, a sting is not a savage act of aggression; rather, it is far more heroic, indicative of a bee's willingness to sacrifice its life to protect home and hearth. That's the bees' reality.

Our Tanzanian beekeepers accept that bees sting and, in a lesson that Winnie the Pooh would surely understand, accept that getting stung is part of getting the honey. In the United States, we would prefer to get our honey from less-threatening bees and to avoid killer bees. That's reality-based living. And reality-based living is, to me, the single biggest factor in remaining secure in an increasingly insecure world.

Reality-based living incorporates our personal reality, which is defined as the way we perceive the world around us. Our personal reality is shaped by our preconceptions, by our experiences, by our paradigms shaped by those experiences, by input from our friends, spouses, and relatives, and by physical surroundings. An example might best illustrate this concept. I live up in the mountains where it snows a lot. Consequently, I spend a lot of time driving in the snow on steep, narrow mountain roads. When my father and his girlfriend visit, if they see one flake of snow at the airport, the thought of getting into a car terrifies them. For people who live in the South, where a couple of inches of snow nearly paralyzes a city, the idea of grinding through the mountains to my house on sheets of slippery white stuff is a very scary personal reality.

If we look at this situation objectively, the reality is that we perceive the snow to be slippery. It is dangerous to drive on. Driving on snow requires specialized skills, specialized equipment, and a higher level of awareness than does cruising down a dry interstate in Kansas.

Reality-based living means stripping away personal preconceptions and analyzing a situation as objectively as possible, then adjusting your awareness, your skills, and your equipment accordingly. Reality-based living requires planning for contingencies so that you can do the things you want to do when you want to do them, like getting home on a snowy evening or collecting delicious honey from a beehive. Reality-based living provides the basis for removing unreasonable fears and accepting the risks associated with everything we do, from our day-to-day urban lives to a hike in the Rockies.

Prey Attracts Predators

Turning now to your preparedness for operating safely in the outdoors, let's consider the perception and the reality of increasing crime in the backcountry. In a sense, those of you who have fears about human predators on the trail closely resemble those Texas farmhands who feared the killer bees. Our goal is to adopt a reality-based-living philosophy and become more like the Tanzanian beekeepers who have found a way to enjoy the treat, be it honey or a glorious spring hike, by developing strategies for obtaining that goal safely.

For many of us, the outdoors has been a refuge, a place to get away from the pressures of the city and the stress of work. Unfortunately, the operative word in this statement is "many." In Colorado's Front Range where I live, five years ago there were hiking trails that only the locals knew about. Five years ago, the idea of traffic jams on many trails seemed ludicrous. Five years ago, the idea that rangers would be ticketing mountain bikers for speeding would have made a great cartoon in a bike magazine. Five years ago, the idea that we might be threatened by the same people we came into the backcountry to escape would get you guffaws at a Sierra Club gathering.

Unfortunately, there are too many of us, and we'd all like to get away from it all. The sheer number of people is attractive prey to some human predators. Click the remote back to one of those 24-hour animal channels, where prides of lions steadily circle huge herds of wildebeests or zebras. Similarly, as flocks of humans have recently taken up hiking, mountain biking, fly fishing, trail running, kayaking, and other outdoor recreational activities, human predators have naturally come along to circle the flocks. And the backcountry is prime hunting territory. Why do I say that? Well, it's the reality of the situation.

For a start, we cannot access telephones on every street corner, where the police are only three digits away. We cannot summon aid quickly or easily; more often than not, we are on our own. It brings to mind the old movie line about space, where no one can hear you scream. The distance from civilization, perceived or actual, further adds to our vulnerability. Predators by their nature like to operate free of restraint. An urban environment puts some level of restraint on law-breakers, as constant crowds of people milling about increase the likelihood of deterring predators.

Also, we've made getting into the backcountry easier and easier. Television, movies, and the advertisement of trendy sports have made activities that were once seen as lifetime vocations more attractive to the average adventurer, and technology has made access easier. The people in charge of our wild places have responded by opening up the outdoors to a level that would have seemed unfathomable 10 years ago.

That being said, the outdoors still calls. There are vistas we want to see, trails we want to hike, and rivers we want to run. There are quiet mornings by a mountain lake and incredible insights discovered leaning against a pinyon pine. We all need to experience this world. That's reality. Sadly, a perception about crime in the outdoors has begun to develop among many people who no longer feel that they can travel in the backcountry safely. Many people are becoming worried about human predators. Whether or not this perception is valid, it is real. Fortunately, you can look at this situation objectively, adjust your skills and your equipment accordingly, and be prepared.

How Do We Keep Ourselves Safe?

So the question becomes simple—how do we keep ourselves safe? The answer is that it's largely in your head. And a lot of it is based on your view of the world.

To create a personally accurate view of the world, you use your experience tempered with awareness. You become attuned to change. You listen to your intuition. You relax and enjoy the world around you while the most powerful tool for safety you possess, your mind, maintains watch. You respect those feelings that we label fear. In short, you don't go into the outdoors blind. Experience, intuition, and awareness are all necessary.

If you live in an urban area you may avoid certain places at night. Perhaps some people have been told that those areas are unsafe. True or false? Who knows? Granted, we usually protect ourselves by avoiding that which we don't know, rather than experiencing it and discovering exactly how much we don't know. Once we have explored these areas, we may realize that these areas are not as dangerous as we perceived them to be. Or perhaps we do encounter a threat. Either way, we strip away the connotations and our preconceptions, step outside our own paradigms, and make our analysis—an action plan—if you will. That's reality-based living.

Can we see the world through completely objective eyes? I doubt it. But each level of preconception we strip away, each paradigm that we're able to step outside of, brings us closer to that ideal.

Think Reality

This afternoon, I'm going snowshoeing. It is 10 degrees outside, and just over a foot of fresh powder covers the ground. The temperature, coupled with the fact that I know I'll be moving, tells me how to dress. The trail I've chosen and the condition of the snow tell me what size snowshoes I should use and how fast I will likely travel. Am I disappointed that I can't move faster? Why should I be? The trail tells me what I need to know. The trail also tells me what I need to know about my personal security, and what precautions, if any, I need to take.

When you plan a trip to the outdoors, think reality. Consider your strengths, your weaknesses, and your level of awareness. You already have the ability to create a mindset that, should you choose to adopt it, can keep you safe in the scariest of environments. Right now, as you sit here reading this book, you have an awesome set of tools at your disposal. You have the ability to read and analyze dangerous situations at lightning speeds and to make decisions that can quickly and effectively take you out of harm's way. You have the ability to be one step ahead of any human predator and to live your life decisively and securely.

These same amazing tools that keep you safe can actually enhance your life. Rather than creating a grinding paranoia that has you always looking over your shoulder, these tools allow you to step outside your fears and see a world more vibrant, more alive than you can imagine. Our first set of tools, which we'll discuss over the next three chapters, is the three-pronged self-defense mechanism, and we'll begin this discussion with an intimate look at intuition. So when you're ready, please prepare for a strange journey into the heart of the very hostile environment of cave diving.

3

Intuition

Hostile Environments

JOIN ME, IF YOU WILL, for a trip to the most dangerous place on earth. No, it's not Los Angeles in high summer or Moscow in the dead of winter. It's not even Kabul, Afghanistan, or Tegucigalpa, Honduras. Join me instead for a trip toward the center of the earth, flying through the great flooded cave systems created by the advance and retreat of glaciers during the Ice Ages.

In an over-saturated media world, where most "extreme" sports that were previously unknown have now become feature programming on many cable television channels, cave diving (scuba diving in underwater caves) remains untouched. For a start, cave divers compose a relatively small group, summing less than 2,000 active divers worldwide. The training for certification is expensive, arduous, and truly spooky, and certification is only a very small beginning. The reason for the sport's exclusivity is simple—if you make a mistake, any mistake, you die horribly in a small, closed room as first your light and then your air run out. Cave diving forces us to look at all the dark, dank crevices in our heads . . . *a fear of being buried alive . . . a fear of suffocating . . . a fear of being trapped . . . a basic childhood fear of the dark.*

I have never been as profoundly terrified as I have been when deep inside a cave. "Are you scared?" my first cave-diving instructor, John Orlowski, asked me in the middle of the grueling certification process.

"Yes," I answered honestly.

"That's the correct answer," he said. "Only a fool wouldn't be afraid in this environment, and I don't dive with fools."

For a human being, an underwater cave presents one of the most hostile environments on earth. You can't even visit there without a complex life-support system, and you can't stay very long without risking your life. Should any small part of your life-support system malfunction, you die. Should *you* malfunction—i.e., panic—you die. Late one night at a dive trade show, a longtime cave-diving instructor (after perhaps more than one beer) remarked wryly that cave diving was the safest sport on earth because, "there are no injuries per 100,000 people."

Let's not study the reasons people are drawn to the underwater mazes, except to say that those reasons aren't particularly different from the reasons you might choose a long, grueling hike—challenge, curiosity, a personal sense of exploration and accomplishment. We currently want to examine the *culture* that cave diving has spawned. The community of cave divers, instructors, and specialty companies that service the sport have established a set of mores—essentially a set of largely unstated rules for survival—in this hostile environment.

The Rules of the Dark Road

Of course there are the basic rules of the road. Every sport has a set of basic rules, and for cave divers, the list is brief:

- Always obtain specialized training.
- Always have a continuous line back to the surface, to the light.
- Always carry three sources of light.
- Always dive at least as conservatively as on the "rule of thirds": use only one third of your air to go in, use one third to come out, and hold one third in reserve for emergencies.

Those of you who are scuba divers have probably already noticed an interesting omission on this list. When a person receives training as an open-water scuba diver, almost the first words out of the instructor's mouth will be "buddy system." The buddy system provides the foundation for recreational diving safety. Scuba divers always dive in pairs, with each buddy looking out for the other. In cave diving, however, divers understand that in this hostile environment, each diver is on his or her own.

If you have a catastrophic malfunction, you have the responsibility for saving yourself. In a cave, as in space or in the Arctic or on a big mountain, a valiant rescue attempt can easily lead to two dead people instead of one. I have seen a person panic in a cave; after that experience, I easily understood where the phrase "out of your mind" comes from. The mind does go away for a while, and a 200-pound thrashing animal pounding itself against a closed-in space replaces the once-rational human being. In my situation, the other person was lucky; amazingly, he got himself back under control. Had he continued to panic, I'm not sure I could have—or would have—stopped him. Simply turning around in the cramped tunnel would have required assuming a contortionist's position. About the most I could have done was hold his shoulders and point my light at my face to show him that I was relatively calm.

When I took my first cave-diving lessons, my instructor showed me a tunnel in a cave that, at its dead end, had gouges cut into the limestone. The fingers of a cave diver had cut the gouges at the end of the diver's life. She had panicked, made a wrong turn down the long, dead-end tunnel, and swam like the crazy person she was at that point. Her husband, diving with her, was left with a choice none of us would want to ever make. He didn't have the air to go after her and survive. His choice was to die with her, or exit.

"He decided," my instructor said with deepening irony, "that it was easier to get a new wife than a new life."

Here's the point: harsh environments tend to create cultures with survival-based rules. The stated and unstated rules of the culture have evolved to help people survive. What might appear strange or even outright crazy to outsiders makes perfect sense within the context of that culture.

The Intuition Connection

Attention to intuition is also characteristic of cave diving. A diver can "call," or cancel, a dive at any point in the dive. I was at a Florida springs once when one of the top cave divers in the world showed up to meet with her team. She'd helped map the very caves we had planned to dive and knew them as well as any person alive. The five divers in her team waited, all fully geared-up and ready to dive. She drove into the dive site in her pickup truck, looked around at her divers, then stuck her arm out the window and gave a "thumbs up" sign, a signal cave divers use to end the dive. Then she headed out for a beer. Everyone began breaking down equipment and packing it up for the day without ever placing a toe in the water.

Was there a little grumbling? Sure, of course. But it wasn't serious grumbling, and nobody said a word to the team leader. Within the culture of cave diving, it's considered the height of bad form to question why a dive is called.

I recall one particular dive with my instructor, John, which was called for no apparent reason. It was a deep dive, bottoming out at almost 200 feet in the cave. The entry had been uneventful; we were swimming against a slight current, which required some effort, but the cave was beautiful. Periodically we passed blind albino crayfish that waved white pincers angrily in our direction. We had dropped into the second level of the cave and were getting ready to drop through a vertical tunnel in the floor of the cave to the third level when John came to a stop, shone his powerful cave light on his hand, and signaled a "thumbs up." We turned around in the narrow tunnel, and I led us back up the line to the surface. We broke the gear down, talked about generalities (usually, in the Florida sinkholes, the talk is about mosquitoes), then headed out for pizza and beer. At the restaurant, John finally decided to break etiquette.

"Normally, I wouldn't say anything about this at all," he started, "but because you're new, I'm going to make an exception. Everything was going fine, but I had this feeling in the back of my head that someone was going to die. The deeper we went, the worse the feeling got. So I called it."

Let's call that feeling in the back of his head *intuition,* and before we talk any more about it, let's jump from the spooky world of underground caves to the warm, homey smells of my grandmother's kitchen.

Mystic Bulletins from Warm Kitchens

I grew up in Tennessee, the Deep South, in the 1950s, and at that time I thought that my grandparents' house was just about the coolest place on earth. Unlike my parents' spanking new house in the suddenly sprung-up suburbs, my grandparents' house was full of old nooks and crannies and a garage full of junk that might as well have been gold. A kid could find lots of things to do in a place like that, and a particularly industrious kid (like me) could do a lot of damage to himself without much effort. Like the time I cut a jagged gash in my arm on a rusted chunk of wagon. Before I had a chance to launch into my histrionics, my grandmother appeared with a warm wet cloth and bandages.

"I'll swanny!" she said (I never did figure out where that particular phrase originated). "I was cooking, and then I just knew that you'd gone and hurt yourself, so I thought I'd better come out to this garage and find you before you screamed and scared the neighbors." The fact that my grandmother arrived before I'd had a chance to call her didn't seem strange to me at all.

Over the years, I quizzed my grandmother about her "feelings," which she never thought of as particularly interesting. She had grown up in a different world, the rural South of the early twentieth century. Times were hard and entertainments few. From these conversations and from my later research for a book on popular culture, I learned that before the advent of mass culture, the South had exhibited a very mystical landscape. The land itself seemed overlaid with its mythic and often bloody past. I experienced this firsthand while standing on an old railroad bridge over the Mississippi near Memphis one foggy night, while my grandfather pointed out where the great Civil War steamboat *Sultana*—the *Titanic* of its day—had exploded and sank, killing hundreds. It seemed as if it had happened just the day before, and as the tendrils of cold fog crept into the dark woods along the banks, I swore I could hear the screams of the injured and see the blood-red glow of the burning ship reflected in the fog. In a culture overlaid with mystical tones, intuition was a natural and accepted part of everyday life.

The Voice in Your Head

A lot of distance lies between the claustrophobic underwater tunnels in Florida and my grandmother's kitchen in the 1950s, but filmy, ethereal wisps we call intuition tie them together. As any number of scientific studies that have focused on intuition over the years have shown, intuition cannot be repeatedly and accurately measured. However, it surely exists. I won't presume to do what decades of scientists have failed to do. But I will tell you that I have learned to listen to the voice in the back of my head.

By way of an introduction to how we can effectively use intuition as a tool, I'll begin with the comparison of the brain's functions to those of a computer. Our brain processes the information that it constantly gathers from all of our senses. Our information-gathering capabilities are prodigious and operate continuously. Like a nuclear version of Microsoft Windows, our brain has hidden capabilities that we can't seem to directly access, or can access only sporadically.

The following story illustrates some of these hidden capabilities. A few years back, I spent some time with a friend of mine who, at that time, was the world-champion practical shooter. As a sport, shooting is incredibly difficult, requiring a very precise muscular trick to align sights, followed by extreme control while pulling the trigger. My friend's particular sport of practical shooting not only requires the precise movements of target shooting, but also includes moving from one shooting position to another. The athlete has to run from position to position—a gross muscular movement—then shift gears into precise muscle control for the actual shot. Courses can take only a few seconds or up to a minute to complete.

I was watching my friend practice a particularly challenging course, using a very precise timer to gauge his performance. At one point he came over to me and said, "You know, Michael, I think I can get four-, maybe six-hundredths of a second off this run." He studied the course for a few minutes, then went back and tried it again. That first run registered a time four-hundredths of a second faster than his previous best run. The next run was five-hundredths faster. The third run was six-hundredths faster, which he then duplicated several times. When he came back over to talk to me again, I asked, "By the way, show me how long a hundredth of a second is."

He looked puzzled, then shrugged his shoulders. "Beats me," he said.

A Question of Software

How long is a hundredth of a second? I don't have a clue, but my brain does. Somewhere buried within software as Byzantine as anything that has come out of the Seattle area in the last few years is an incredibly efficient timer—a timer that not only can keep tabs of infinitesimal increments, but can also reprogram the gross muscle functions of the body to speed them up. If you ever get the opportunity, go for a run with an Olympic-level runner (if you can convince them to slow down for you!). As you're running along, ask him or her about the details of your pace. You'll be amazed at the level of detail you'll get.

During conscious activities, our brain gathers information from every source it has available to it and, in the background, processes that information and runs it through a set of filters of which we're only vaguely aware. Occasionally, that background processing kicks up a piece of information that our conscious self needs—immediately. Intuition is one of those instant messages from the computer-processing center in the back room, e-mail from the back of our head.

"Something's come up, and here's a suggested course of action."

We live in a culture that—despite a fascination with the non-measurable tasks our brain performs—doesn't put a premium on intuitive action. Say, for instance, you get up tomorrow morning and feel a little "hinky" about the day. You call your boss and say you won't be in, not because you're sick but because of that "hinky" feeling. As they say in the movies, "Forget about it!"

Let's think about that for a minute. Cultures that have developed in hostile environments tend to place a premium on, as my cave-diving instructor says, "stuff that keeps you alive." Whether we look at ancient native populations or today's high-tech alpinists or divers, we see cultures that value the voice in the back of the head, e-mail from the lower brain. Yet the culture in which we all presently live tends to dismiss those feelings outright.

Internal Back Talk

Say you've embarked on a weekend hike along California's Pacific Crest Trail. The weather has been perfect, the scenery grand. You don't even have a single blister. About midday on Saturday, you pass an obviously illegal campsite; the messy remains of a fire pit sit just a couple of feet off the trail. You stop, pick up the litter and cover the unsightly fire pit, mumbling about the inconsideration of some people. A few hours later you hike past three young men sitting on a boulder in the sun passing around a bottle. They are cordial, even friendly. But you immediately get a "ding" in your head—you've got mail. And we all know what that mail says—*Danger! Danger! Danger!*

Before that mail can get through to the intended recipient (our body) and generate the expected response (preparation to either flee or fight) the mail gets intercepted. Our conscious mind steps in and, like a school crossing guard, raises a hand and shouts, "Halt!"

"Let's," says our conscious mind, "examine this piece of overwrought mail."

What have the young men actually done?

Nothing.

Have they been courteous?

Absolutely.

Have they been threatening in any way?

Nope.

Didn't you leave CNN on all day while you packed so all the bad news that's fit to air subliminally trickled into your head?

It's important to be informed . . .

And look, they're members of a different race. Might some unconscious racism be at work here?

Well, it's not impossible...
And didn't you have a tiff with your husband before you started out Friday morning, and might you be tarring *all* men with the same brush?

Maybe...
And isn't it after noon and you haven't had a bite to eat?

Yes...
And your blood sugar has bottomed out, and you're parched, and they're laughing and drinking a beer...

True.
"So," your conscious mind says triumphantly, "that explains everything. That e-mail ding is clearly the result of a hungry, thirsty, pissed-at-the-Spousal-Unit overreaction, guiltily fueled by lingering racism and too much CNN. So there!"

Not only have you successfully talked yourself into ignoring your intuition, you now feel slightly guilty for even having it, as if your unconscious mind, totally without your knowledge or approval, has rummaged around in the closet of your unconscious and pulled out all the embarrassing photos. And if you happen to pass another group of young men along the trail, the mental conversation shortens still.

Ding!
"Shut up—we've been through this already."

The Parrots' Lesson

We mentally reward ourselves for triumphing over our animal instincts. Let's isolate the animal instinct further; what would an *animal* have done in the same situation?

I share a house with two large parrots; an African gray named Ripley and a blue-and-gold macaw named Cleo. Unlike dogs and cats, parrots don't have a millennium of history as domestic animals. Rather, these relatively wild animals have entered into an uneasy relationship with their human keepers. Parrots possess extreme intelligence; some long-term university studies indicate that parrots may be among the most intelligent animals on the planet. The studies also suggest that by our own human standards, parrots have the ability to reason. Prodigious intelligence aside, however, in their native habitats, parrots are *prey* animals— other animals, and sometimes people, eat them.

From watching my own birds, I've isolated Parrot Rule Number One: *When in doubt, fly.*

They process their e-mail very differently than we process our e-mail. Their internal conversation appears more like this:

Ding!

"Fly!"

Although parrots have some impressive tools with which to fight—a beak, for example, that can neatly clip a small steel bar in two or quickly reduce a chunk of lumber into a pile of wood chips—the first *intuitive response* is to remove themselves from the threat. Parrots are intelligent and have created a model that can be helpful to humans as well as parrots.

A friend of mine, one of those old raft guides who should know better but doesn't give a damn, decided to float a portion of the Rio Grande through Big Bend Park in a single raft with his partner. Without any other company. Having never been down the river. So, at the outset we're dealing with an individual who has violated more rules about conducting safe outdoor trips and river safety than we need detail here. His reality? He'd had years of experience throughout the world on white-water rivers. He had planned for the trip for several months, and he took a partner who was equally qualified and understood the risks. His major concern? Humans. The Rio Grande is a major smuggling route into the United States, and smugglers can be, when surprised, notoriously ill mannered. His solution? Avoidance and awareness.

One night, after several hours of rowing in nasty, cloudy weather, he and his partner arrived at their planned campsite. They were tired, hungry, and ready for food and sleep. Night was approaching. They tied off the raft, set up the tent, and started to prepare supper. But it just didn't feel right. *Ding!* "Fly." They spent the night in another campsite with cold food, less sleep than they'd want, and a few cross words. Yet overall the trip was wonderful. My friend experienced vistas, canyons, and a glorious river with days of no human contact. Was there danger that night? Who knows? But they safely completed an adventure of a lifetime with planning and an understanding of the reality that existed at that time and at that place. They utilized their intuitive messages and maintained an awareness of their environment. Their awareness helped them respond to their intuition appropriately.

However, as we will see in the next chapter, developing awareness does not always come naturally.

4

Awareness

The Ballad of the Clueless Poacher

I ONCE HAD THE UNPLEASANT EXPERIENCE of watching a poacher work his way through a national forest.

I was writing an article on "fast-packing," a buzzword for hiking really fast, for *Men's Journal* magazine. Because the article was on a crash deadline—aren't they all—I decided to head for someplace close to home, the San Juan Mountains of southern Colorado. With the exception of a few well-publicized trails, the San Juan Mountains don't have the kind of hiker traffic you might see closer to Rocky Mountain National Park, although the vistas are every bit as spectacular. My partner, photographer Denise Jackson, and I decided to dodge the late-season snow and stick to the lower trails. We were a few hours into our hike, moving very quickly with daypacks only, when both of us froze.

Above us, your basic camo-clad guy with a shotgun moved through the trees. We stepped back off the trail to watch. All hunting seasons were closed (we'd checked before we hit the trail), and he was on a well-marked hiking trail in a national forest. That made him, by definition, a bad guy. Aside from the fact that nothing repulses me quite so much as a poacher, I was struck by how clueless he actually was. Although he displayed a television version of stalking—his head swiveling back and forth with slow, measured movements—he didn't actually seem to *notice* anything.

Myself and my partner, for instance. Or the herd of mule deer, including two small bucks, which were also standing off to the side watching the "hunter" hunt. I had this vision of the whole San Juan Mountain ecosystem standing off to the side, waiting for our clueless poacher to open his eyes.

An interesting and complex situation had arisen here. The poacher was doing all the "right stuff," but was totally unaware of his environment. Denise and I maintained awareness of the poacher and the deer. Our reality featured a bad guy who didn't know what he was doing. A bad guy who could, intentionally or unintentionally, fire at us as sure as he could fire at the deer. We had ratcheted up our awareness and tailored an action plan that required us to really blend into the background. The deer's reality? *Ding!* "Fly." Quietly. The poacher moved on, we moved quietly in the other direction, and the deer lived another day. However, what if we had viewed the environment as the poacher did, and the poacher had had our view of reality?

Keen Observers

I've never met anyone who didn't think that he or she was a keen observer of the world; in other words, that he or she was *aware*. Here's a quick quiz—stop where you are right now, close your eyes, and mentally write down a detailed description of your immediate environment. This exercise may remind you of those tests in popular magazines of whether, at this moment, you can remember what color shirt your boyfriend wore this morning or the style of your wife's earrings when she left the house for work. If you complete this mental note-taking honestly, you'll realize just how little we actually notice in the course of our day. We think we are completely aware of what's going on around us; in fact, we probably take in less than 10 percent of the stimuli in our world.

Why does this occur?

Well, I'm not going to delve into any deep Eastern thought about how we, as Westerners, find it difficult to live in the moment. In my travels, I've met my share of oblivious Easterners as well. Rather, I'd like to look at our lack of awareness from a distinctly Western, that is, a very deterministic perspective.

We are, as are all animals, partially products of our environment, and our environment is fairly nuts. A few years back, many stories and studies centered on the subject of "information overload"—I even wrote a few of them myself. The basic thesis stated that, thanks to our knowledge technology, our personal environments had become increasingly dense. We had simply been, and continue to be, exposed to a continually expanding amount of input. A walk down a crowded urban street generates a staggering amount of sensory input—noise, smells, sights, the jostling of other people, the traffic just a few inches away. Television, radio, movies, and the Internet all scream for our attention. Plus, we are suddenly being forced to process more information and to process it much faster. Speed, I teach in my business seminars, is the defining word of the new millennium.

Speed and overload have implications for the way our brains process information as well as for the way business is done. You'll notice that the media coverage of information overload has diminished these days, and I think that's because, for all intents and purposes, we've given up. Our over-stimulated sensory environment has won. We deal with our personal defeat through the creation of mental filters. We build these filters totally unconsciously, and we use them in the same way and for the same reason that we use telephone answering machines—to screen out unwanted "calls." So when we walk down a trail crowded with other hikers, we may be totally aware of, say, a striking member of the opposite sex, while totally unable to recall a fork in the trail that we just passed. How powerful are these filters? More powerful than you can imagine.

The Hidden World of Paradigms

A few years back, I had the privilege of working with a business consultant named Joel Arthur Barker. Barker popularized the concept of "paradigms," by his definition, the rule-set by which we view our world. Barker contended that businesses often blind themselves to new opportunities by being trapped in their paradigms, unable to see what, in retrospect, would be opportunity knocking. Barker used the classic business example of the Swiss watch industry. Prior to cheap digital watches, the Swiss watchmakers ruled the roost, controlling something like 70 percent of the worldwide market for watches. Amazingly, Swiss industry researchers actually invented digital watch technology, then literally gave it away because they didn't see any value in it.

A watch was a timepiece, an heirloom, and a once-in-a-lifetime buy. It wasn't a piece of cheap junk with a chip in it. Of course, it turned out that people didn't want an expensive heirloom; they just wanted to know what time it was. The Swiss watch industry nearly collapsed amidst the tidal wave of cheap digital watches produced for this market.

However, the Swiss did have the last laugh (proving that they learned quickly and could abandon paradigms) when they roared back with "fashion" watches—buy a bunch, one for each outfit—effectively shattering the paradigm that a person might need only one or two watches.

In an effort to demonstrate our personal paradigms, Barker developed a series of experiments. One of Barker's experiments involved scuba divers. He took a plain old red Coca-Cola can down 50 feet or so underwater, then sent divers down to look at the can. When the divers came up, Barker asked them a simple question—what color was the Coke can? Without exception, the divers confirmed that the can was *red*. One small problem here—color constitutes a reflection of a specific wavelength of light. The wavelength of light that we define as *red* doesn't penetrate that deeply through water. It was physically impossible for the can to be red, because, at that depth, red doesn't exist. The can was white. Even upon repeated questioning, the divers insisted that they had seen a red can.

Barker then created another, less-wet test. This time, he had a special deck of cards made. The hearts and diamonds of Barker's deck were black instead of red; the spades and clubs were red instead of black. The simple experiment entailed quickly showing people a card and asking them what color it was. Barker found that more than 80 percent of the people tested insisted that hearts and diamonds were red and spades and clubs were black.

Barker concluded that our filters are so powerful that they can actually work in reverse and tell us what we experience. The divers "saw" a red Coke can, even though the can should have appeared white, because somewhere in their brain a usually handy filter says, "Coke cans are red, silly." Our experimental card players "saw" black spades and red hearts because they had their own set of filters that says, "Spades = black and hearts = red."

Blinded by the Filters

Barker's groundbreaking research boils down into two primary points:

- We unconsciously create powerful filters that help us sort through the information overload around us.
- These powerful filters can actually dictate what we see; that is, we see what we expect to see.

Our clueless poacher *thought* he was keenly observing his surroundings. But, his observations were consciously and unconsciously filtered in such a way that he was obviously unaware of his surroundings. The fact that we have these filters that stand between the real world and our perception of that world creates the first problem with awareness.

A second problem with awareness arises in the form of the "point man syndrome." You've all seen war movies where a small group of men move through a jungle, fearful of contact with the enemy. A soldier up front, the point man, always leads the way. The point man sweats bullets, his eyes jump nervously, every muscle in his body remains tense. In our terms, he's manually overridden all the filters; he's reached back into his head and turned the knobs labeled "sensory input" up to maximum; he is as alert, as *aware*, as a human being can be. And why not? People, in fact, plan to kill him and his friends. For the point man there is no mercy, no quarter, and no room for mistakes. However, the point man is also *tired*, really tired. Heightened awareness requires more energy than normal, just as a three-position flashlight burns longer in the "low" position than in the "brightest" position. Yes, we can manually override our filtering system, but not for long.

If you want to give yourself quick proof of this, sign up for a mountain bike downhill race, such as the legendary Mammoth Mountain Kamikaze Downhill in California. When you manage to hit around 50 miles per hour on a mountain bike, your sensory apparatus, fueled by "flee or fight" blood chemistry, cranks wide open. Things happen very quickly, and the consequences of making a mistake include the loss of a lot of skin or a long, long flight off the edge of a cliff. Plus, it's a race; you're right out there on the edge of your abilities, pushing the personal envelope.

Pushing the Envelope

The first time I did Mammoth—a race way beyond my limited ability at that time—when I got to the bottom of the mountain, it was all I could do to get off the bike, sit down, and allow my blood chemistry to return to normal. Then I packed up my bike, went back to the hotel, and slept like a stone for about five hours. I had just experienced 100 percent awareness for about seven minutes.

My fatigue did not result just from the physical exertion of the race. I had also expended an incredible amount of mental energy. Total awareness while participating in any outdoor activity requires both physical and mental energy.

Total awareness makes your body and your brain tired. Total awareness uses energy. And energy is a limited resource. In order to raise our awareness of our environment, we need to override our own filtering system. But that requires energy, both physical and mental.

We can best utilize our energy by reprogramming our filters to serve us rather than blind us. Reprogramming of filters is accomplished first by becoming more cognizant of our awareness and then by learning to tailor our awareness to the given situation.

How do we become more cognizant of our awareness? This question isn't one of those Zen conundrums. Quite simply, we become more cognizant of our awareness in the same way we become more cognizant of anything: by paying attention to it. Remember the first time you went on a hike with a real woods person; remember how amazed you were at how much that person saw; remember seeing all the flora and fauna that were previously invisible to you. And recall the next time you went hiking in the same area and how much more you saw just because you paid attention to it.

Next time you go for a walk down a trail, or are out on a run, stop and ask yourself, "What am I aware of? What's going on around me?" Don't make it a long stop. It's more of a quick bulletin. Then move on. In about 15 minutes or so, do it again. Now think about what you're doing here. You're telling your brain that paying attention to your environment is important. A brain is a quick study. If you explain to it what you actually want it to do, you'll be surprised at how quickly it picks up on it. Therefore, the first part of the reprogramming process is letting your brain know what's important to you.

You've now told your brain that you want it to pay

attention to your environment. But remember that heightened awareness takes more energy and you may need that energy for other tasks. You actually want your brain to shift gears from one level of awareness to another, whenever the environment around you changes. That way you can keep yourself at the lowest, safe level of awareness for as long as possible and use as little energy as possible.

You can accomplish this quick switch in gears by giving your brain a shortcut, a mnemonic device to assist you so that you don't expend precious energy every time a change in your environment occurs. Let's go back to our analogy of the brain as a computer. Database searches work most effectively when the search criteria is as specific and restricted as possible, right? When we say we need "increased awareness," our brain is forced to perform an extremely complex search. Suppose, though, we predefine different states of awareness, then assign each of those states of awareness a specific name or, in our case, a *color*?

True Colors

The Awareness Color Code was developed by military and police organizations and is quite a useful tool. Let's take four colors—white, green, yellow, and red. The color *white* means that you're totally unaware of what is going on around you. The color *green* means that you're in a relaxed state of awareness. You're paying attention, and nothing in the environment sends up an alarm. The color *yellow* means that something about the environment has pricked your senses. You're suddenly much more attentive. The color *red* means that you are now in a critical situation. You must be fully alert and ready to respond.

The military and police utilize a fifth color, by the way,

one that I hope you'll never have to call up on your mental computer. Condition Black means you are involved in a self-defense, potentially life-threatening situation. For many police special teams, Condition Black means that the shooting has started.

Sadly, most people spend their lives in Condition White, unaware of everything. Those at this awareness level will run into you on the sidewalk, then seem surprised and angry that you got in their way. They will cut you off in traffic, then give you the old "one-finger salute" in a fit of rage. Here's an example from the outdoors. In 1995 I made an unsuccessful attempt to summit Mt. McKinley, Denali, in Alaska, the highest mountain in North America. Denali can present many faces to climbers, some benign, some deadly. One thing has remained consistent over the years on what the Native Americans called "the Great One"—for every 100 people who attempt to summit, on average one climber fails to return. Some years are better, some years are worse, but the great mountain always extracts its toll.

The team I was with was descending from Camp 5, which nestled into the base of the mountain's headwall, through a section of rock-hard blue ice. To our left was a jumble of ice boulders; to our right, across the shining blue field of ice, was about 2,000 feet of drop. Slip, be unable to find purchase for your ax in the hard ice, and you take the long ride down.

Needless to say, my team stepped carefully. Amazingly, we were passed by a young couple—arguing. They shouted at each other, gesturing angrily with their ice axes. Their rope hung slack between them, virtually guaranteeing that if one fell, the other would be unable to hold the fall as his or her partner rocketed toward the abyss. To get around us and another team descending with us, the couple looped far out onto the steeper, untracked ice. My team leader called an immediate halt—"If they go," he said, "I don't want to see it." We all agreed.

That, folks, is Condition White!

Being Green

I contend that we go into the outdoors in order to experience the outdoors; we should *always* be in Condition Green, a relaxed awareness of our environment. We want to see the fawn and its mother, almost invisible at the edge of the trail; we want to see the golden eagle on the hunt, the high alpine flowers hiding in the lee of the boulders, the fat marmot watching us from the edge of its domain. Just as importantly, we have an interest in the signs on the trail that tell us what's ahead, and provide us with clues about what we'll be face around the next bend. In this, we don't particularly differ from any other animal, predator or prey, as we try to read as much of the terrain as we can.

What I see might bump my state of awareness up a notch. Mountain biking in the Colorado Front Range last year, a friend and I came across a patch of fresh mountain lion tracks on a sandy stretch of ground. I quickly ratcheted up my awareness from Condition Green to Condition Yellow; I wanted to pay attention to everything. I didn't progress to Condition Red, however, because no threat had actually materialized. The lion had clearly been there, but that's all we could honestly say. I did look ahead, however, and saw that the trail dropped into a little draw, shaded by overhanging rocks... perfect hunting territory for a lion. I suggested we take a branch of the trail that climbed through open country. This constitutes *strategic* thinking; my general strategy in lion country prescribes that I avoid making myself attractive Lion Chow. By sticking to the general No-Lion-Chow strategy, I changed my own plans and wished the King or Queen good hunting.

And after a few minutes of riding on the new trail branch, I dropped back into Condition Green. What would have happened if we had come face-to-face with the Lion King or Queen? Straight to Condition Red!

I would go to maximum awareness. From a biochemistry perspective, various arcane chemicals would pour into my bloodstream, getting me ready to flee or fight. My vision and hearing would have narrowed and tunneled, allowing me to clearly pinpoint the threat. My body's operating system doesn't care that the threat is standing in front of me and growling and that I need to think, not just flee or fight. I get the whole chemical package.

If I am to successfully avoid being the feline equivalent of a TV dinner, I first have to conquer my own blood chemistry. Our amazingly powerful flee-or-fight software and its associated chemical factory generally come in handy in the evolutionary scheme of things. But with only two choices—flee or fight—our operating system software doesn't always address complex situations. For example, in my present situation, if I flee, the lion will tackle me in about two small bounds. If I am unarmed and I stand and fight, the lion, arguably one of the most sophisticated killing machines on the planet, will get the decision by a knockout in the first round.

Clearly, I need another program up and running. To do that, I need the ability to think. In order to think, I need first to quiet the chemical rush in my head. In Condition Red, I shift from *strategic* to *tactical* thinking. *Where's my best exit? What do I need to do to make the lion think I'm bigger and badder than I really am? What if I threw my bike at the lion? Is there a big stick close by? Can I use my cell phone to call for help?*

In the bout between Michael and the Lion, thinking my way out provides my only chance of victory. Not so far-fetched a solution, considering we are the most successful animal to ever walk this planet, and our single overwhelming advantage is our brain. Br'er Lion has it all over us in terms of sheer strength, speed, skills, senses, and armament, but look how few hikers actually end up the victims of lion attacks in an average year—one, two, some years none at all.

Feline Wisdom

Before we move on to the next point, let me make one thing very clear. This book isn't about being safe from lions; it's about being safe from people. In fact, lions need protection from us rather than the other way around. But I used, however unfairly, Br'er Lion in the above scenario because I wanted you to think about *being confronted by a predator.* Because some humans on the trail are exactly that: predators.

How do we accomplish the reprogramming of our filters to serve us instead of hinder us? Our minds will do what we tell them to do, if we remember to tell them anything at all. Examine how quickly we program ourselves with negative information—*I can't do this.* I once read that it only takes a couple of midnight runs to the refrigerator fishing out that errant pint of Phishfood ice cream to "program" your mind to wake you up at 3 A.M. and announce, "Wow, I'm hungry!"

You start reprogramming your mind by simply telling it what you expect from it—in this case, you expect your mind to raise your awareness level in response to your intuitive

feelings about your environment. When you feel the necessity to raise your level of awareness, stop and make a mental note that, "This is Condition Yellow." Keep mentally
annotating your level of awareness. You will quickly teach
your mind what you mean by each level of awareness, then
you will file that information away. Eventually, you'll
remind yourself that you should be in Condition Green, and
your mind will know exactly what you mean and respond
accordingly. This reprogramming will allow you to use your
much-needed energy for important things, from enjoying the
scenery to surviving a potentially violent situation.

5

Fear

Things That Go Bump in the Night

UP TO THIS POINT we've dealt with reality, intuition, and awareness. As you move into any environment, as you begin that weekend hike in the Appalachians, you need to have created the best view of reality that you can, and you need to utilize awareness and intuition. Further, you need to know when to be afraid. A powerful emotion, fear can like all emotions, help you or cripple you.

After one of my business talks about the fascinating and very real relationship between high-risk sports and strategic business planning, a young female executive whom we'll call Anna pulled me aside and said she wanted to ask me a couple of questions.

"Sure," I said, and we walked off to get a cup of coffee. Anna had some troubling questions. "I want," she began, "to talk about fear. In your speech, you kept talking about fear as if it were an old friend. I just kept thinking that this guy has a personal relationship with fear."

I nodded in response to her perception. "But that's not what fear is like at all," she continued. "Fear is this awful thing that never goes away. It's like a disease you can't get rid of. I know fear, and I hate it and wish it would go away."

A long, rambling narrative followed revealing that a close friend of Anna's had been raped, and the rapist had succeeded in injecting a toxic level of fear into both Anna's life and her friend's life. Her friend's rape, and Anna's own perceived vulnerability, ran like a steady drone in the back of Anna's head—when she walked to her car at night, when she ran in the mornings, when she went on business trips to new cities.

"So you're telling me that fear is a *tool*," she concluded, "and I'm telling you that fear is a *disease*. What's the deal?" The question gave me pause. The fear of rape is clearly not irrational; however, the irrational fear of rape is irrational. Rape is, I believe, the single greatest security risk facing women. However, I do not believe that women should let the fear of rape define the parameters of their lives. I do not think anyone should live with irrational fear, that is, fear not connected to any specific risk factors.

Is Fear a Disease?

As humans we know some concepts so well that we don't think we need a working definition—I'm *happy*; I'm *angry*; I'm *afraid*. While we certainly all experience these emotions—happiness, anger, and fear— (along with, I believe, much of the animal world), we certainly don't share a consensus about what they mean. One person might correlate happiness with the moment of a child's birth. A different person might associate the same emotion with successfully screwing a competitor in a business deal. These feelings, these emotions are, by definition, subjective.

We could stop right here, and just say that since emotions are subjective, we don't need to delve any deeper. However, if we are going to be safe in the outdoors we must embrace fear. Fear is not only part of our "early warning system," but is, in fact, one third of our most basic self-defense mechanism.

We began by looking at *intuition*, and how we can begin to rely on the machinery of intuition to help us make decisions. We next explored *awareness*, so that we might understand how awareness works as part of our "programming toolkit." Awareness programs the software in our mind so that we can positively react to changing environments. Now we come to the third part of the equation.

What is *fear*?

I define fear as a specialized subset of intuition designed to warn us of imminent danger. If you happen to be, say, out on the trail doing research for an article on fast-packing and, unbeknownst to you, you are being stalked by a poacher, it becomes vitally important that you immediately pay attention to any e-mail from the back of your head.

Nobody explains fear as well as Gavin de Becker (one of the foremost security consultants in the world) in his classic book, *The Gift of Fear*. "Like every creature, you can know when you are in the presence of danger," he writes. "You have the gift of a brilliant internal guardian standing ready to warn you of any hazards and guide you through risky situations."

Fear, then, is a warning system—*You're in danger! Stand by and prepare a response!*

When we go into the backcountry, we need our warning system to operate 100 percent accurately. In the backcountry, we do not have the same ability to predict aberrant behavior as we would in an urban setting. In *The Gift of Fear,* De Becker outlines his premise that violence, which we normally think of as random and unpredictable, exhibits neither of these characteristics. By understanding that violence is generally not random and is generally predictable, and by trusting our instincts and paying attention, we can remove ourselves from the path of most violent events and violent people. From my own experience, I tend to agree with him. I think that violence resembles a summer thunderstorm—quick building, incredibly powerful, and, in most cases, predictable. Problematically, prediction requires contact, at some level, with that which you're going to predict. If you're trying to predict who might stalk you, for instance, you need to have had some contact, however small, with the potential stalkers.

Most of us haven't had prior experience or contact with human predators in the backcountry. Crimes in the backcountry tend to be exceptions to the old police truism that most crimes of violence occur between acquaintances. Crimes in the backcountry tend to resemble classic crimes of opportunity. Criminals—predators—intend to rob or commit an act of violence upon someone, but that someone isn't necessarily you.

Our goal involves removing the "necessarily" from the statement made above and guaranteeing, as much as possible, that you are not a victim. To accomplish this we must make sure our intuition-awareness-fear subroutines work properly. Fear is not an absolute; fear, like intuition and awareness, is programmed and programmable. Granted, we probably have some built-in fears. I have read that most animals, humans included, display a reflexive fear of snakes. When I performed an experiment on one of my parrots to test this theory, he did indeed recoil in apparent fear from the fake snake that I presented, then struck hard with his powerful beak. However, when he realized that the snake was a harmless piece of rope, he reprogrammed himself to simply ignore future "snakes."

Fear can arrive in response to very specific stimuli, a guy running toward you brandishing a baseball bat, for instance, or to more general circumstances, like a bad workplace situation. Recall the example above with the poacher closing in? It's unlikely that the person hiking felt "fear" because the article on fast-packing might not be completed on deadline; maybe anxiety, if the magazine editor was a tyrant. In a situation where your life is at risk, fear is useful only insomuch as it is a true warning. *A poacher is closing in* is critical life-or-death information; *I might miss my deadline* isn't.

Unfortunately, our present culture allows real sloppiness when it comes to our fear. We fear lots of things. According to Barry Glassner in his book, *The Culture of Fear*, we fear all the wrong things—killer diseases, feral youths, psychotic parents, airplane crashes, deadly gasses seeping up from the basement, runaway drug abuse, road rage, cyberpredators—you name it, we fear it. As Glassner correctly points out, this generalized cloud of fear blinds us to real fear.

"We had better learn to doubt our inflated fears before they destroy us," he writes. "Valid fears have their place; they cue us to danger. False and overdrawn fears only cause hardship... I do not contend, as did President Roosevelt in 1933, that 'The only thing we have to fear is fear itself.' My point is that we often fear the wrong things."

Mental Car Alarms

Our overuse of fear closely resembles our society's reaction to car alarms. Remember when the first car alarms appeared? When a car alarm went off, people actually—brace yourself for a shock—went outside to see what was wrong! Amazing! The car alarm went off, and people responded quickly! What happens when a car alarm goes off today? Do people jump up from their seats and race outside to see if a car is actually being stolen? Are the phone lines flooded with people calling 911? Do police cars screech to a halt beside the noisy vehicle?

Recently, on a trip to New York City, I heard a car alarm go off. The alarm did not stop. Eventually, a neighborhood resident dropped a concrete block through the windshield to remind the owner to get an alarm with an automatic shutoff. Fairy tales do indeed come true—cry wolf too many times, and nobody will respond when the wolves are actually at the door. If we fear too many things, our brains will not react satisfactorily when real danger confronts us.

Let's revisit Anna, the woman at the beginning of this chapter. Anna tries to listen to her intuition, but the noise factor is too loud. She's afraid all the time, so how can she realize when a real warning comes in? Bringing our intuition-awareness-fear subroutines into the correct balance requires us to turn down the noise.

If we are going to turn down the noise we must remember that formless fears are just that, formless. They generally don't hold up when exposed to the light of our awareness. We must start examining our underlying pool of fears and evaluating them. Obvious examples include the generalized fears that are pounded into our heads every night on the evening news. If we really examine, for example, flesh-eating bacteria, we'll see that the likelihood that we'll suffer from exposure to such bacteria approaches the likelihood that we'll be struck by lightning on the day we win the lottery.

Glassner, in *The Culture of Fear*, researched the presence of road rage, a very popular modern fear. It must be sweeping the country, he theorized, since it seems to be on every television show and in every newspaper and magazine. Yet Glassner didn't find the hard evidence to back up the hype. In fact, compared to a real killer like drunk driving, road rage is just a tiny footnote.

Anna did indeed have a valid concern—rape. But was the fear of rape justified? Not at the level at which she experienced the fear.

Fear Functions

Fear, to serve as nature intended, must be *specific*. "At this place, at this time, I am afraid." My subconscious, my intuition, which has access to tons more information than my conscious does, is sending me a one-word e-mail that says, "Danger!" True fear is the smoke alarm in your head going off, and, like that screaming smoke alarm, it *demands* a response. It doesn't necessarily demand an *action*, by the way, but we'll get to that in a minute.

In Anna's case she must replace her nebulous concept of generalized fear with the Awareness Color Code:

Condition White
Condition Green
Condition Yellow
Condition Red

The fear of rape is a valid fear, but rapists don't lurk everywhere. Anna would honestly be at greater risk in certain places. Let's go through a few scenarios to see how it works:

Eating lunch in the building cafeteria... *Condition Green*, walking around the neighborhood in the daylight... *Condition Green*, walking across a large, empty parking lot at the airport... *Condition Yellow*, seeing a single male loitering at the corner of that same parking lot... *Condition Red!* A response is necessary. In this particular case, the response takes the form of an action—go back inside the terminal.

I tend to talk continually to my subconscious, letting it know what I expect of the internal software. For example, I might tell my subconscious not to bother me with a fear alert when I walk into a darkened parking lot; I might just raise my awareness to the peak of yellow. I don't need to be afraid; I need to be aware. I then trust my intuition to send me a fear message when it's truly necessary. True fear provides us with an early warning.

There are some environments where fear is the only rational response. As my first cave-diving instructor said, "If you're not afraid in the caves, I won't dive with you." The same goes for being on a big mountain in a screaming blizzard, at least for me. So how do we deal with fear when it is the correct response?

The Continuum of Fear

When fear demands a response, that response isn't necessarily an action. We don't always need to flee or fight. Sometimes, before fear becomes overwhelming, we need to think.

Fear, like awareness, is a continuum. We can progress quite quickly from being slightly afraid right up to absolutely stone-cold, deer-in-the-headlights terrified. In at least one way, fear reminds me of my parrot Ripley. When he asks for something the first time, he tends to use a reasonable voice. By about the tenth time, if I continue to ignore him, he can shatter glass. Fear is an emergency call, and if we ignore it, our subconscious turns up the volume. And don't forget that our subconscious controls a huge chemical factory with which it can make its point. If we ignore our fear, it returns more powerfully than ever. When the fear volume reaches a peak, we can get one of two responses:

- Paralysis, the classic deer-in-the-headlights syndrome, or
- Panic, manifested in aimless running, screaming, what have you.

Neither of these responses is conducive to survival, since they both shut down our most important survival tool—our brain. We don't have three-inch claws, long, sharp teeth, or even the ability to leap tall buildings in a single bound. All we have is our brains, and that's been enough to put us on top of the evolutionary cycle of this planet. As Aikido master George Leonard pointed out in his moving book, *Mastery*, we are the most successful predators to ever roam the planet. That is, when our primary tool is working. In order to deal with many fearful situations, we must acknowledge our fear and set aside the "flee or fight" reaction. We must be able to gather and analyze data and formulate our options.

Strategic and Tactical Thinking

When you recognize fear, your thinking should shift from strategic to tactical. For our purposes, strategic information is information generated in a planning process coupled with a notion of what we aim to accomplish. Strategic information provides a basic outline for action—"If it rains I'm going to make camp rather than push on." Conversely, tactical information is real-time information that facilitates action on a specific point. Tactical information helps us create options for action, within our strategic plan, based on real-world, real-time data.

To illustrate, our strategic plan for handling conflicts on the trail is "Avoidance of a potentially dangerous encounter." Assume you have already gotten a "ding" from your intuition. You have jacked up your awareness, acknowledged and set aside your fear, and now have shifted to tactical thinking: "I know from my planning that the trail in front of me narrows and dips down through a small canyon. If I go into that canyon, I'm going to have limited options for either escape or evasive actions. There's a campsite about 100 yards back with a couple of tents set up by a stream. Rather than go on, I think I'll go back to that campsite and have lunch by the stream and give those suspicious bikers I just saw an hour or so to pass."

Tactical information answers the questions:

1. *What is my situation right now?*
2. *What is my risk exposure right now?*
3. *What are my options for action right now?*

In short, I want situation evaluations and alternatives— exactly the same thing that Captain Kirk always wanted when the Enterprise got smacked by a photon torpedo. Unfortunately, I don't have Spock, Scotty, and Bones to report to me; I'm doing all the reporting. Also remember in those Star Trek episodes that Kirk never said, "I'll need those evaluations when you guys get around to it, but don't knock yourself out." What Kirk was always shouting was, "Now!" And that's the mode you must be in. Tactical information constantly updates. Tactical situations are fluid, and I want to always be open to changes in my tactics that can get me through the unfolding situation unscathed.

We will be talking more about tactical thinking and what to do if you find yourself involved in a violent encounter; however, in order to complete our strategic plan, we must first discuss two practical topics: the completion of a risk assessment and the information-gathering process of planning.

6

Completing a Risk Assessment

Risky Business

A CRUCIAL STEP IN PREPARING A STRATEGIC PLAN for any safe recreational trip in the backcountry is the creation of a risk assessment. Before we get into the details of this exercise, however, we need to understand some basics about what the term "risk" actually means.

Back in the 1960s, classic science-fiction author Ray Bradbury wrote a story called "The Naming of Names." I read the story at the age of 14, at which time I also had an English teacher who spent hours hammering into us the necessity for precision in our use of language. From my English teacher and from Ray Bradbury, I learned that names, and words in general, carry incredible weight. By naming a thing, we attempt to nail it into place, to slip it into a pigeonhole where we can quickly understand it without having to go through a lengthy thought process. For example, when presented with the phrase "Yellowstone Park," the brain kicks up a shorthand version or picture of what we think of as Yellowstone Park. Words are the keystrokes with which we program our subconscious routines. I didn't pay much attention to this lesson until years later, when it occurred to me that, sticks and stones aside, what you don't understand can kill you.

Neuro-Linguistic Programming

A few years back, an investment group came to me and asked me to help launch a magazine on "the self-esteem industry." How much, the investors asked me, did I know about the self-esteem industry? "Well," I answered truthfully, "until you asked, I'd didn't know there *was* a self-esteem industry." I had this momentary mental picture of a self-esteem assembly line, with smiling people putting together happy faces and sending them on down the line. Despite this hokey vision, I agreed to give the project a try.

Soon afterward, I discovered one discipline within the self-esteem industry called "neuro-linguistic programming," on which a tremendous amount of research had been done. The field deals primarily with the way we assign words and pictures to ideas and experiences in our subconscious mind. Neuro-linguistic programmers assert that we constantly reprogram our subconscious, usually without intent or direction. For example, if a student says he's going to do poorly on an exam, he probably will because his subconscious has picked up his words and used them to program his mind. I had a friend who would get up every morning and exhort, "Well, another crappy day!" Not surprisingly, he had a lot more crappy days than great days.

This book attempts to take the precepts of neuro-linguistic programming and apply them in a very practical manner for the specific goal of personal safety. Neuro-linguistic programming has been used for other practical purposes such as the elimination of stage fright, allergies, and other pesky problems; it has also been used in the field of psychology to treat mental disorders stemming from major traumas or abuse. Neuro-linguistic programming has additionally been used for frivolous matters, such as the one below, which I find quite amusing.

As the editor of the esteem magazine, I once went to a seminar on verbal programming and visualization featuring one of the experts in the field of neuro-linguistic programming. He was indeed a wonderful speaker, awing the audience while he explained how to program yourself to get a Cadillac. According to his plan, every morning you would get up and say, "I am a Cadillac owner!" Maybe you would put some yellow Post-It notes on your refrigerator that read, "I deserve my Cadillac!" Then, to help you visualize yourself in your Cadillac, you would go down to the Cadillac dealer, ask to demo the Cadillac of your dreams, and have your picture taken in it. The picture would go right up on the refrigerator next to the Post-It notes. In no time at all, you'd be cruising in your Coupe DeVille.

Well, maybe.

If you want a Cadillac, I'd suggest a second job or rich relatives. But neuro-linguistic programming works amazingly well (and quickly) for purposes such as ours. Hopefully, after the last few chapters, you've made the first tentative steps toward reprogramming your head for your own safety. You've stopped talking back to your intuition, you've started building your Awareness Color Code, and you've taken the first steps to understand and use your powerful fear alarm. Now we will apply a similar process to our concept of "risk" to ensure our brain kicks up an accurate picture in response to the word.

The shorthand notations we assign to a word tend to shape our whole view of what the word actually means. It's back to that paradigm thing—the shorthand notation we attach to the word becomes our reality.

But what if our shorthand notation doesn't give us *all* the information we need? This may not pose a big problem if the word is "detergent;" however, it may pose a really big problem if the word is "risk." Therefore, your next step in living strategically and feeling secure is understanding risk, and you can't take that step until we have a common language.

What Is Risk?

The best definition of "risk" I've found comes from a white-water rafter: "Risk is the increased consequence of failure." If you fall out of a raft in Class II water, you get wet, but if you fall out of a raft in Class V water, you can get dead. We can conclude accordingly that the consequences of failure increase drastically from Class II to Class V rapids. An activity, then, might be said to increase in risk as the consequences of failure increase.

From that definition, we evolve the concept of risk factors. A risk factor is something that increases the consequences of failure. Hiking, camping, and just being in the backcountry are pretty safe activities, especially compared to something like cave diving or driving on the Los Angeles freeway system. When we go into the backcountry, though, certain factors do cause our risk—the increased consequences of failure—to increase.

How about this list:
• Proximity to cities

- Size of our group
- The composition of our group
- The presence of alcohol or drugs
- Economic condition of the surrounding area
- How far we are from "civilization"

Each of these factors adds a little to our level of risk. The closer we are to a major city, the easier it is for a human predator to get out on the trail. An individual is more vulnerable than a group. A small group is more vulnerable than a big group. A group made up of college students looking to party runs a greater risk than a group of dedicated long-distance hikers or adventure racers. And do you really need me to tell you that puffing on that big old joint while dogging it down the trail—and, folks, I see this all the time here in the heart of the Rocky Mountain High—increases risk? If the surrounding area is economically depressed—not uncommon in many rural areas—all that natty Patagonia outerwear is going to look mighty tempting to a potential thief. Finally, the farther we get from civilization, the more the constraints of living in a civilized manner loosen on some individuals.

Evaluating Risk Factors

Two distinctions affect the concept of risk, and we need to address both before we can pull together an accurate risk assessment. First, we must understand the difference between a "perceived" risk and an "actual" risk.

As an illustration, a couple of years ago I wrote a book that served as an introduction to scuba diving. In the course of writing the book, I talked to dozens and dozens of new divers. As part of my interview process, I asked each one of them to describe the risks associated with diving. Without exception, they all mentioned some variation of "getting eaten by a great big fish" as one of the top three or four risk factors.

Could you be eaten by a big fish when scuba diving? Yes, and as I've mentioned, you could also be struck by lightning on the day you win the lottery. Realistically, unless you smear yourself with bacon fat and insist on diving off Catalina Island in the middle of the night, you're not going to get eaten by a shark. Attacks by sharks, crazed barracuda, giant squid, and other assorted denizens of the deep fall into the category of "perceived" risks. If you're a diver, the over-whelming number one *actual* risk factor is nitrogen, which you absorb into your bloodstream as you descend and which must boil out of your blood as you go return to the surface. If you fail to off-gas nitrogen slowly as you ascend, you can end up in a hospital, in a wheelchair, or in a coffin.

Now, which risk factor do you think you should spend the most time on, understanding nitrogen or learning how to avoid sharks? The question is germane because until we clearly understand which risks are actual and which risks are simply perceived, we might be tempted to devote time, which is a limited resource, trying to protect ourselves from things that aren't likely to happen. Think that's far-fetched? I sat in one basic scuba class years ago where shark avoid-ance actually got *more* time than dealing with nitrogen.

I like the way cave divers handle the perceived-versus-actual debate—they define an actual risk as that which is most likely to kill you. To avoid that risk, discover what you must do 100 percent right, 100 percent of the time, then learn to do that very well.

The second distinction concerning risk follows directly from the perceived-versus-actual discussion. We must establish whether a risk is "objective" or "subjective." The following explanation is my bastardization of some mountaineering thinking: A subjective risk is a risk factor over which you have some control; an objective risk is when God points at you and says, "You're it."

To me, coldness is a subjective risk—I can control what I wear, or what I carry as backup. My physical condition, which is a risk factor during an arduous endurance-demanding event, is definitely under my control. An avalanche, on the other hand, is largely caused by the finger of God. All I can do is try to understand why avalanches occur and try to arrange my life so I am not in the range of an avalanche when it comes down. Obviously, these are not super clearcut distinctions, but they help you start thinking in the right direction.

Risk Assessment 101

When we evaluate risk factors, we begin creating a basic risk assessment. Whether we call it that or not, we all do some sort of risk assessment whenever we consider taking part in various activities. For example, "Taking a bicycle tour of South Central Los Angeles doesn't seem like such a great idea." Or, "Gosh, a long hike around that steaming volcano in Mexico may not work out well." Or, "A camping trip to a popular family area where there has just been a string of car break-ins just doesn't seem wise."

Risk assessment is fundamental to living strategically. For every trip I take, I put together some form of risk assessment. If I'm climbing a 14'er in Colorado, the risk assessment might be quick and informal as I am very familiar with the area—I might consider the possibilities of afternoon thunderstorms, crowded trails, and vandalism in the parking area. If I'm considering a trip out of the country, Denise and I will spend a good bit of time crafting the risk assessment.

We must set aside a portion of time to assess risks. We can do it formally, by sitting down with a pencil and paper and making a list, or informally, by keeping the list in our heads. I suggest doing it formally, with pencil and paper, especially at first. If you like, use the following sample risk assessment as a guide for completing a trip-specific risk assessment:

A CHECKLIST FOR RISK ASSESSMENT ON THE TRAIL

1. How far are you from the closest urban area? "Close" tends to suggest a higher risk.
2. How large is that urban area? "Big" suggests a higher risk. A hiking trail near Los Angeles is proportionately more dangerous than a hiking trail near St. George, Utah.
3. How heavily traveled is the area you are visiting/hiking/ biking? More traffic might suggest a lower risk factor, due to the proximity of people and the ability to join a safe group if necessary.
4. Did your research turn up any reports of crimes within the target area?
5. Did your discussions with locals turn up any anecdotal information on crimes in the area?
6. Are you traveling alone?
7. How big is your group?
8. What is the composition of your group?
9. What best describes the economic strata of the area you travel through?
10. How long will you be out on the trail?
11. How far will you stray from the trailhead and from your

car, which is always an attractive vehicle for escape?
12. Do you plan to travel at night?
13. How would you describe the topography of the area you'll travel through? Open? Forested? Above the tree-line? Take a few minutes to think like a criminal. What would you like if you were planning to rob someone?
14. How heavily burdened are you? This will indicate what your level of fatigue is likely to be and how quickly you can run like hell if necessary.
15. What is your level of fitness? Again, fatigue increases risk; the better shape you're in, the better able you'll be to respond to a developing situation.
16. Do you have any specific self-defense skills? Martial arts, counter-rape training (the Model Mugging program, for example), boxing, and other training might fall into this category.
17. Are you armed and *trained*?

To summarize, the goal of the risk assessment is to understand the actual risks, control what you can control, and don't agonize about the rest of it. I have been in the woods with people who obsessed about everything. What about snakes? What about bears? What about blizzards? What about e-coli? What about those Crips and Bloods who are out for a holiday in the country? A risk assessment helps you avoid those unfounded worries, or at least allows you to answer all your nervous friends' questions.

However, there are actual risks of being on a long trail, and there are actual risks associated with taking a dayhike. There are actual risks associated with almost any outdoor activity. How do you start rounding up the information that helps you intelligently make your risk assessment? You plan.

7

Planning

The Unsexy Stuff

PLANNING AIN'T SEXY. In fact, according to some of my friends here in the Colorado Front Range, it's downright boring. In fact, they think that *not* planning is essential to spontaneity. They think that the more we plan, the less spontaneous we are, and heading into the backcountry should be an act of spontaneous joy. I have a different view; of course, our various excursions into nature should bring us joy, and sometimes surprise adds to the bliss. However, as you'll learn in this chapter, going through a planning process coupled with a risk assessment can actually allow you to extract *more* of that wonderful spontaneity, as you'll arm yourself with knowledge that encourages safe flexibility within the risks of each situation.

Six Steps for Planning Outrageous Trips

In my business speeches and seminars, I outline the six steps that I've used to put together some fairly scary trips (and some pretty mundane ones as well). Some of these steps will serve to refresh your memory from earlier chapters, while a couple of them now demand further exploration:

1. *Choose a summit.* A summit, as opposed to a goal, has the power to capture a person's soul. I have found that people are more likely to accomplish an outrageous goal (such as climbing a 20,000-foot peak) than they are to reach a more attainable one (like losing 5 pounds).

2. *Abandon your comfort zone.* This one is tricky. The very subject this book tackles causes discomfort. However, if you never abandon this zone, nothing exciting will ever happen to you! When planning a trip or event, I make a conscious effort to keep a distance from my comfort zone and explore.

3. *Narrow your focus.* In a sense, adjusting your levels of awareness accomplishes this. Moving up through the awareness scale narrows the focus. In a similar fashion, you should ensure that your vision for the trip or event is sufficiently narrow to allow for specific planning.

4. *Understand the risk.* This includes understanding the distinction between subjective versus objective risks and perceived versus actual risks.

5. *When in doubt, go faster.* This is counter to basic intuition, as humans have a reflexive urge to MOVE . . . STOP . . . EVALUATE . . . MOVE AGAIN. Unfortunately, in a high-risk environment, this puts you at a much greater risk than continually moving. This is also true in a self-defense situation, where fluid movement is often the key

to escaping the risk or even to survival. Part of planning involves preparing yourself for such a situation.

6. *Embrace chaos.* Survival in a "chaos system" demands research, and this is where the real work of planning begins.

Embracing Chaos

For our purposes, we define a "chaos system" as one in which unforeseen and unforeseeable consequences result from small non-repeating activities. In other words, stuff happens, and we're not sure why. The exact same set of circumstances might not yield the same results twice. In a normal environment, we would put systems into place to keep things we don't want to happen from happening again. We call this root cause analysis—we go back and fix the cause so that the result won't trouble us again. In a chaos system, though, we can't find the root cause, or if we do find it, it doesn't matter because what happened was a unique event. It follows one of those pesky laws of thermodynamics: in any system, entropy increases. As soon as things begin, things start falling apart.

Nature is the ultimate chaos system. When we head out on the trail, literally millions of factors act on us. Each combination of factors is unique, and the consequences of those factors acting on us are both unforeseen and unforeseeable. However, all is not lost. You can employ the following steps to help you survive in and embrace a chaos system:

- Recognize that you are in a chaos system.
- Beware of self-limiting paradigms.
- Control what you can control.
- Think flexibly.

Recognizing the Chaos System

We often have trouble believing we're in a chaos system because we like to be in control. Control contributes to our basic comfort zone. As a writer for *Mad Magazine* once noted, "I am the master of my fate; I am the captain of my volleyball team." One of the basic catch phrases of our culture is, "Relax . . . it's under control." However, violence is a chaos system! In a violent confrontation, you are not and cannot be in control!

Yes, on television and in the movies, action heroes both male and female always seem to be in cool control. In a real violent confrontation, there are too many factors outside your view, too many unknowns, too many combinations, and too many unforeseen outcomes for you to be in control. Therefore, you must relinquish this wish to be in control; you will then have the ability to act within the parameters of the situation without needless panicking.

Beware of Self-Limiting Paradigms

Secondly, there's the problem of paradigms, our personal set of constructs that shape how we see the world. These paradigms can blind us to potential harm if we let them. I had an opportunity to learn this lesson during my years in the martial arts. Tang Soo Do, a Korean form of karate, features high, sweeping kicks and elaborate moves. After spending several years studying Tang Soo Do, I met a former Navy Golden Gloves boxer who told me an interesting fact. "Korean guys are easy to knock down," he told me, "once you know the hole in the system." He proceeded to show me "the hole in the system," which involved first distracting the opponent, then feigning a sweeping, round kick, and finally delivering a simple, direct punch to the jaw. After getting knocked to the ground, I rose groggily to my feet, rubbing my jaw.

"The problem with karate man," my witty Golden Gloves champ explained while I shook the stars out of my head, "is that he thinks he knows what's going to happen. He's spent years watching for that little shift in the hips, that cocking for the kick. He sees that, and his whole body sets up to block and counter the kick. Except the kick doesn't come." He grinned.

To counteract the possibility of being surprised in this manner, the only defense you have is acute awareness of your environment and of your personal paradigms.

Control What You Can Control: Developing a Planning Strategy

Of course, no amount of planning can prepare you for those events outside of your control. However, knowing what the subjective and objective risks are, and therefore what you *can* control, allows you to begin developing a planning strategy. To be sure, everyone plans his or her trips to some extent. You want to know roughly where you're going and what you're going to do. But the planning I have in mind is more than a simple itinerary. Rather, I hope to collect as much information as possible to plug into my risk assessment. The more information I possess, the more accurate the risk assessment becomes.

I initially encountered serious information gathering in preparation for my first international trip with my partner, Denise. As a professional photographer, Denise had traveled solo extensively in Africa and Russia (not known as great places for a woman traveling alone) and never experienced a bit of trouble. That was because, she claimed,

when she was out of the country, she always stuck to Third World Rules. Her rules had never been written down, but their basic outline went something like this:
1. Know as much as you can before you leave
2. Keep your head down (don't draw attention to yourself)
3. Don't ever drink the water.

The rules have changed and evolved over the years, but they remain the basis for safe travel. Since the most important rule is by far the first, having a good planning strategy is crucial.

Appropriate Levels of Planning

I think of every major trip as a research project. In my own planning, I consider any trip to be "major" if I plan to go into territory I'm not familiar with, if I plan to stay out overnight or longer, or if I plan to leave the United States. This definition encompasses a fairly broad spectrum of trips; however, in the case of planning, I'd always rather err on the side of too much rather than too little. Minor trips are also subject to information gathering, although not necessarily at the level of that for a major trip.

The Research Process

Information gathering starts with guidebooks. For a major trip, such as a multi-day hike on the Appalachian or Pacific Crest trails, I expect to spend several hours at a bookstore comparing guidebooks. I'm lucky enough to live near Boulder, Colorado, where local bookstores sport aisle after aisle of guidebooks. Look for bookstores in your area that carry a wide selection of guidebooks and begin frequenting them. Big outdoor retailers, such as REI and Eastern Mountain Sports, also carry a great selection of guidebooks. In addition, independent outdoor specialty retailers also take pride in their book selection.

At this point, I'm just gathering data and starting to put together a quick mental picture of the trail—how many miles am I looking at in total; what's a rational expectation of the number of miles per day; how should I classify the difficulty of the trail. Eventually, I'll purchase, borrow, or checkout two or three of the guidebooks I like the best. It's important to remember that *some guidebooks have errors,* minor or otherwise. Also, all guidebook writers have their own quirks and their own criteria for ranking difficulty, enjoyment, and amenity. For example, the various guides to hiking in Rocky Mountain National Park describe the trek up Long's Peak, the highest mountain in northern Colorado, as anything from a fun dayhike to a really scary scramble. The truth is, as you might expect, somewhere in the middle. However, buried in those guides is the tidbit of information that all the books have in common—for example, that the final approach to the summit is steep, exposed and, in wet or snowy weather, dangerous. That's the tidbit of information you're looking for.

Sometimes authors of guidebooks have a specific audience in mind for their material. This approach can be very effective and efficient. However, some such guidebooks are aimed at trekkers with about 50 cents in their pockets. I've seen some recommended hostels in various countries that I wouldn't stay in with an Uzi and a detachment of armed guards. This risk makes it important to check out the criteria used in the guidebook, line it up against your own criteria, and evaluate whether or not the guidebook will provide you with information that you personally feel is valuable.

On a foreign trip, once I arrive in a country, I always like to spot-check the information in my guidebooks by cruising by a few places the guidebook recommends (hostels, campsites, trailheads, and so on) just to get a feel. If I get bad e-mail from the back of my head, I downgrade the guidebook in general.

I like topographical (or "topo") maps, too. Between the guidebooks and the topo maps, I'm constantly creating a mental image of the trip. I match the descriptions in the guidebooks with the terrain of the topo map, and I try to visualize the lay of the trail. I ask myself some fundamental questions that will help me to assess risk—Am I going to be on my hands and knees at any point? Where would be a good place to finish for the day? Is the area heavily forested? And so on. Topo maps are included in many good guidebooks, and you can also purchase them separately in map sections of large bookstores or outdoor retailers.

Throughout this research process, I'm looking for any data that can be pasted into my basic risk assessment such as, "There has been lots of vandalism in the trailhead parking lot," or "Don't leave anything valuable in your car." Such comments raise small red flags. When the book was written, enough of a problem existed so as to encourage the writer to flag the issue. Apparently, a few of the local predators had already figured out that hikers or mountain bikers were relatively easy targets. As I've mentioned before, popular trails are more crowded today than they were just two years ago; trails that were secret two years ago have been discovered and publicized in this month's *Bike* magazine. Therefore, if a guidebook made reference to problems when the book was written, I make the assumption that the situation is either the same or that it has worsened since the book's publication.

For planning purposes, we need to think like a scuba diver. Divers tend to round off numbers to give them a higher safety margin when determining how long they can safely stay underwater: 10.8 minutes of bottom time becomes only 10 minutes of bottom time. Similarly, if you make an assumption, always assume in the direction of a greater safety margin.

Fleshing Out the Picture

Once I have this basic picture of my trip in place, I want to throw the net a little wider. Using Internet search engines, I start looking for any magazine articles or newspaper pieces written about the specific area I'm visiting. If any violent incidences in the particular area I'm going to have occurred, those incidences usually turn up. At the very least, I'm getting a more detailed picture of where I'm going and what I'm going to be doing. Searching the Internet is an art, and— honest disclosure—in our partnership, Denise usually adopts the role of the searcher. She has a knack for finding tidbits of information, then following the tidbit back to its original source to determine whether or not it can be relied upon.

Outdoor sports and adventure websites can also provide valuable information for planning various trips. Many of these sites allow you to ask questions, which get answered directly by some really excellent outdoors-people. Use these sites—more data is better. If I'm going out of the country, I hit the U.S. State Department advisory site (http://travel. state.gov) to see if our tax dollars at work have coughed up any interesting information.

Red Flags

The more red flags I get, the deeper I go diving for information. If I see a red flag in any of my Internet information

—an article on a violent incident, a reference to a violent incident, or a warning of any kind—I go to the next level of gathering data: interviewing. I start calling around, looking for people who have been to where I'm going and can give me some direct information. I level with them about what I'm looking for: "I saw an article in such-and-such magazine about a rape along the trail, and I was wondering what it was like when you were there . . . anything spooky? Crowded?" Whatever information I can get is factored into my risk assessment.

Throughout the planning process, I'm going through my risk definitions—perceived versus actual; subjective versus objective—and I'm plugging in the data. Once I have a risk assessment that makes sense to me, I start planning to minimize my exposure to the risks.

Planning In Action

To demonstrate this entire process, let me give you an example from a trip on which Denise and I embarked last year. For *Men's Fitness* magazine, Denise and I went to Mexico to climb Pico de Orizaba, an 18,701-foot volcano situated about four hours from Mexico City. We began our planning exactly as I described above, at the local bookstore. We found one climbing guidebook on the volcano itself and several guides we'd used before on Mexico City and central Mexico. We gathered up the guidebooks and did a rough cut of the trip itself. Since we didn't want to put together the logistics of the climb ourselves, we decided to make arrangements with a climbing tour group and "tag onto" one of the their guided climbs. After a quick surf on the Internet, we had a list of all the guide services running trips on the volcanoes. Our first choice was Mountain Travel•Sobek (MTS), whom we'd both worked with before. With a few phone calls and some judicious whining, we managed to attach ourselves to a two-week trip that culminated with the climb of Orizaba. At our request, MTS forwarded to us tons of information on the climb and the area of Mexico in which we planned to travel.

We knew that we would have several acclimatization days in Mexico City before we actually joined the MTS group. We figured that once we were attached to the group, we could focus on the climb itself, which seemed fairly straightforward. In the meantime, we focused on outlining the dangers in Mexico City. Our first Internet searches threw up a major red flag. A *Wall Street Journal* article outlined increasing crime problems facing Americans in the Mexico City area. According to the U.S. State Department, as many as 50 percent of the ubiquitous green-and-white Volkswagen taxis, which turn the largest city in the world into a game of pedestrian polo, are driven by bandits looking for smiling, happy tourists to rob.

Several days of research, a return to the bookstore for yet another guidebook and a transit map of Mexico City, and a bunch of hours on the Internet yielded such tidbits as how to safely pick a taxi, which areas of town to avoid at which times, train and bus schedules (including, oddly enough, which buses featured American movies), and many other safety-related items. This information in hand, we headed off to Mexico, and the trip went off without a hitch. We knew where we were staying. We knew where the bus station was in relation to where we were staying. We knew how to hail a legitimate taxi. We had a rough idea of what we wanted to do each day and how we might go about doing it. Because we had the center of the city nailed down, we were able to slip away for side trips, explore different areas, and, in general, play the tourists. We had a great time, climbed a mountain, ate some delicious mole sauce, and cruised home, all within the realm of safety.

Information on the Ground

On a hiking, biking, or climbing trip, we always augment our research with information found "on the ground." When we get to a new place, before we head out on the trail, we hit a couple of local shops and ask questions. For example: "Anything we should know about such-and-such trail? How's the weather? What are the demographics of the people we might encounter here or there?" We do anything we can to supplement what we already know (or think we know). Frequently, we stumble across local guidebooks that don't make it to national bookstores, or even www.Amazon.com, which we add to our collection.

Think Flexibly

That brings us to the final step for surviving within a chaos system—maintaining flexibility. The level of basic planning which I've engaged in actually gives me a *greater* ability to be flexible, because I have something on which to base my flexibility. A military saying goes something to the effect of, "No battle plan ever survives its first encounter with the enemy." No plan ever goes off without a hitch—ever. In fact, I expect that my plan will not survive intact, but so what? Remember the risk assessment—we know what are actual risks, and we know the risks over which we have some control. Informed risk assessment gives us the flexibility and ability to do what we want to do how we want to do it. And what could provide more joyful spontaneity?

8

Violent Encounters

Strategic Thinking

SO NOW YOU'RE FEELING FAIRLY PREPARED for your next outdoor adventure, right? You've been working on your intuition-awareness-fear mechanism and have started to
reprogram your brain to respond appropriately to changes
in the environment. You have also learned to create a com-
prehensive risk assessment and are eager to fill it with lots of
juicy information gained through painstaking research.
You've got brainpower and practical exercises on your side.

But what will you do if, despite all that planning, you are
actually faced with a violent situation? We will pursue the
answer to this question for the remainder of the book, as we
examine different options for resolving violent encounters,
and the order in which those options should be considered
and acted upon. In this chapter, we'll shift from thinking to

doing, and, unfortunately, that transition can be a little unsettling. I hope that, by this point, you're starting to see that strategic thinking and its attendant mental programming is a way of life, not a trick to protect yourself at a specific time and a specific place. Even with years of training and preparation for dealing with criminals, people can still find themselves reacting in less than optimal ways to their assailants if they do not listen to their fear in time.

On this morning's television wasteland, I watched an interview with a former police officer who had left the force to teach women self-defense. She spoke of a defining point in her life when, while she was off duty, a man stuck a gun in her back and said, "Your money or your life," or something to that effect. She did what most people would do in that situation. She froze. Despite the police training, despite mentally addressing the multitude of what-ifs that being a police officer could demand of her, she froze. So she decided, quite bravely I think, to spend the rest of her life studying our old friend "Fear" and teaching others to do so as well. She had recognized that her fear was the element which had caused her mental processes to break down, rendering her unable to take any action. And she did not want to be in that position again.

Fear, panic, and escalation of force all contribute to a failure to live *strategically*. They represent a shutdown of our thinking processes. Attempting to deal with fear, panic, or the escalation of force while simultaneously trying to think clearly and rationally is kind of like driving on ice. A couple of years back, I took a class on ice driving up in Canada; it turned out to be lots of fun as long as it was someone else's BMW. I learned, among other things, that cars, when they're on ice, are not really very good at doing more than one thing at a time. You can brake. You can steer. But you can't brake and steer (or steer and brake, for that matter). When you attempt to steer and brake at the same time, you actually end up doing neither. Instead, you slide out of control. It's an apt metaphor. Fear or panic or escalation of force is sort of like braking. Thinking is sort of like steering. If we try to do them at the same time we tend to skid uncontrollably, neither slowing down nor going in the direction we'd hoped.

Escalation of Force

Notice that I include escalation of force right up there with panic and fear. Panic often creates an escalation of force, causing us to become our own worst enemies. Because we don't understand the concepts of escalation of force, we often act as the force escalators at the very time we should be de-escalating.

The first riot I was ever involved in—the middle of which was chaos, pure and simple—provides an example of the patterns created by force escalation. It was the last aboveground action of the Weathermen, an assault on the South Vietnamese Embassy in Washington D.C. at the height of the Vietnam War. Cars burned as people pounded mounted police officers with chains; it was an incredible melee. However, the more I watched from my vantage point behind a barricade of garbage cans, the more I noticed that little patterns swirled around in the chaos.

I believe that all violent encounters, although rooted in chaos, have very specific patterns. The most important pattern for us is the escalation of force. Not in every case, but in most of the situations we'll encounter, force will ride an escalator up and up, driven by small actions or thoughtless words on the part of all participants. So what are our options when faced with such an escalating situation?

A Self-Defense Strategy

Andrew Branca, a Massachusetts attorney, is one of the most thoughtful writers on self-defense issues around. His book, *The Law of Self-Defense*, is a dense, legal-reference-packed study of what self-defense law actually means. In the postscript to his book, Branca outlines his own personal self-defense strategy, and I think it's worth reproducing here. A self-defense strategy should form part of our overall package of trip strategies. We've planned for our transportation, our gear, our food, and the weather; we also need to plan for our self-defense. Branca's "decision tree" provides a place to start. The "decision tree" lays out his strategy, in a branching decision-making structure, for dealing with any potentially violent encounter. If the first response doesn't resolve the situation, you move on to the next response, and so on through the decision tree. Although he doesn't explicitly say so, the self-defense strategy, like all our strategies, remains a basic blueprint, a best-case scenario; the blueprint will be filled in by real-world tactical data as it arises.

Branca's six-point strategy follows, where the responses to the violent encounter are listed in order of utilization:

1. Avoid
2. Placate
3. Non-Lethal Options
4. Retreat
5. Presentation
6. Engage

Notice that Branca's decision tree follows a logical sequence, matching a rising crest of escalation. Also notice that Branca's strategy arises from a specific philosophy, which loosely states, "I don't want to hurt anyone." In order to avoid hurting anyone unnecessarily, we must establish answers to the strategic questions we'll encounter when we won't have time to thoroughly think them through. To answer these questions, we must define our limits.

Defining Our Limits

When we talk about self-defense, we must hammer out our own personal limits. The exercise of defining limits will kick out different answers for everyone, and these limits contribute fundamentally to our subconscious programming. The absolute worst time to have this conversation with your subconscious is when you're standing on a trail, your daypack in your hand, facing a couple of individuals who profoundly frighten you. So you must now ask yourself:

What are your limits?
To what extent will you go to protect yourself?

These are the hardest questions in this book and they come at this point because, up until now, all the information and tools I've presented are designed to keep you *out* of trouble in the first place. The intuition-awareness-fear tools are useful whether you're at home watching "When Good Pets Go Bad" or slogging along the Pacific Crest Trail. Avoidance, as a concept, works as well in the grocery store parking lot as it does in a campground at midnight. However, we now cross an invisible line when we start thinking about what we'll do when trouble actually approaches— when we hover on the edge of Condition Black, when our bodies flood with "flee or fight" chemistry, when the fear alarm hammers in our heads.

High-risk sports teach us that we must answer those questions in advance of the event, not during the event. Let's say I'm going to jump off a cliff with a parapente (similar to a paraglider). Before I make that jump, I methodically consider each move in my head, each step I'm going to take. Then I do a quick what-if analysis and establish options for escaping possible failure. I'm doing all the headwork now because once the process starts, once I actually start running toward the cliff with this ridiculous parachute-thing over my head, I no longer have the time to process information through the front part of my brain. When I am speeding toward a 1,500-foot cliff from about 20 feet away, I do not have the luxury of unlimited time to process, "Gee, I tripped over that rock . . . I wonder if I really am this adventurous . . . what will I do if . . . should I stop or keep going or try to pull the wing down or . . . *ahhhhhhhhhhhhhhhh!*"

As humans, we have the ability to make lightning-fast decisions, but not if we have to run the thoughts through our reasoning processes. Instead, we have to short-circuit the decision-making process, use our preplanned model, and route everything through our "lizard" brain, the older, prehistoric part of our thinking machine more concerned with survival issues than with Mozart. The effective functioning of that lightning-fast process depends on intelligent programming, including answering all the strategic questions in advance.

Working Within the Framework

We want our subconscious to be programmed to respond in any way it can while remaining within our basic strategic framework. Our strategic framework resembles the paths through the water sought out in white-water kayaking.

When a kayaker scouts an unfamiliar river, he or she looks for a line through the rapids, a best-case route through the waves and the water. In essence, the kayaker thinks, "If I do everything right, and the river cooperates, this represents the best route to take down the river."

Of course, not just one line exists through a set of rapids. A best line might emerge, but lots of other lines through the rapids will present themselves, and if we screw up, or if the river throws us a little curve we're not expecting, we're going to discover those other lines. On the river, as in life, we need to react, respond, and keep our head above water. I once did a television segment on river surfing, which is basically white-water kayaking without the kayak. The river had dropped a foot from the time I had scouted it in the late afternoon to the next morning's film session, so I knew I was in for a bouncy ride—sort of like sitting in a washing machine filled with rocks. During my first run for the cameras, I hit my line perfectly. On my second run, I bounced one time too many and missed my entry into a small water-fall. Suffice to say that I discovered many other lines through the rapids! However, my preplanning included a safety kayaker downstream whose whole purpose in life was to bail me out if I signaled—strategic thinking!

Our strategy for self-defense acts as our line through the rapids of life. We follow it as best we can, and we build in the mental flexibility to survive when we miss that narrow entry into a waterfall. I once read an article that described our thinking processes in terms of index cards. We create an index card for each anticipated situation, so that when that situation happens—Whoops! Missed entry to waterfall!—our brain searches for the appropriate index card, on which is printed the correct, or best, response.

Unfortunately, this approach is a little too mechanistic and limited for our strategic lives. We simply cannot have enough index cards to address any and every situation we might come upon. Instead, we need to access our strategic model and our most powerful self-defense tool, our brain. So that our brains will be most effective, we must prepare ourselves as much as possible for the unexpected. This means it is critical for us to keep surprise to a minimum.

Surprise

Wait a minute, you say, everybody gets surprised. Look at that female cop—she got surprised, and she was highly trained. You've got to be crazy to talk about not getting surprised, and so on. True, everybody gets surprised once in a while. However, ending up in a disadvantaged position due to being surprised is not entirely out of our control. I define "surprise" as the complete failure of two of our three early warning systems—awareness and intuition. I strive, and I hope you'll strive too, to be aware (that is, in Condition Green or higher) all the time. I want to see clearly what happens in the world around me. In addition to noticing the expansive beauty and blessings around me (which are many), I want to be aware of any unpleasant situations that develop as well. I also hope that my intuitive abilities add to my security. I hope that e-mails flow from the back of my head on a regular basis, and that I act on those e-mail bulletins. If those two early warning systems are in place, things will surprise you a lot less than they would have in your pre-strategic life.

I have spent many, many days hiking, biking, rafting, kayaking, climbing, or participating in other outdoor pursuits. I can safely conclude that you're less likely to be caught off guard in the outdoors than you are at a New York City deli. The outdoors provides open space. We can often see what's ahead of us and what's behind us. The very factors that tend to make us more vulnerable—the fact that we're farther from civilization, for example—can also work in our favor. We might not be able to carefully analyze every person we pass in our New York deli, but we can very probably study the people we pass on the trail in detail. We have more luxury to study our environment through the planning we perform, and that allows us to minimize the element of surprise and to think rather than react.

What Are Your Limits?

To review our scheme so far, when confronted with a violent situation, we can refer back to our self-defense strategy and work within its framework. We can maintain our intuition and awareness so as to minimize the possibility of being surprised, and thus respond more quickly and appropriately. And we have asked ourselves the questions:

What are my limits?
To what extent will I go to protect myself?

What are your limits? I can't answer this question for you. I can't offer you any shortcuts, any mnemonic tools. None of us likes thinking about this stuff, because it punctures our security balloon; it makes us address the thorny issue of our own mortality. When someone wants to hurt us, to kill us, what are we willing to do? It reminds us that while Hannibal Lector is the stuff of fiction, Ted Bundy walked among us. It forces us to look at the question asked by the child in the second Aliens movie: "Mommy and Daddy said there were no monsters. Why did they lie?"

It's not enough to think that you sort of know what you're willing to do when faced with a serious threat. I've had literally hundreds of discussions about self-defense with people from all stripes of life. Most of the people I've talked to have mentally hedged on the question. They say, "Well, I think I'd be willing to do... but only if... and under these circumstances... maybe... or maybe not." Once you cross the border from Condition Red to Condition Black, you will not have the time or the available RAM to answer these questions, or to further refine your answer. Once you enter a situation with a predator, all your mental processes must be used to process tactical information. It's no different in the high-risk sports arena. When you're cave diving and, after a good smack on a rock wall, your primary regulator stops working, you do not have the time to think, "Gee, is cave diving a good idea? Maybe I should take up golf." You fix the problem, or you die. I can tell you my own answers, but in the end, you're going to have to do your own agonizing.

Predators

As you formulate your answers to the serious questions above about what you will do in a situation that escalates to violence, you must consider the person you will confront. As discussed previously, crimes in the backcountry are most often not perpetrated by friends or relatives of their victims.

What we are dealing with here are predators. Click back to the 24-hour animal channel and check out those lions circling the wildebeests. The stalking of the lions has nothing to do with compassion, with an urge to better the herd, with altruism of any sort. Those lions constantly weigh risk versus reward. Is dinner worth a kick to the head? Well, that depends on how hungry Ms. Lion is. And, of course, whether Mr. Wildebeest looks like he can deliver a good, solid kick to the head of a hungry lioness.

The best description of human predators I've ever read comes from ex-Secret Service agent Walt Rauch in his book, *Real World Survival: What Has Worked For Me*:

> "This guy is not your next door neighbor, your lodge brother, your golfing buddy, or fellow church member. Although he is a member of the human race, he doesn't share any of the same moral values that you hold. He has no qualms about his actions in rape, robbery, murder, or any other action that is devastating to you. He is not easily frightened, if at all, or deterred from his goals. He understands violence very well, for it is one of his predatory survival tools. He is goal-oriented and will not desist in his actions unless the cost appears to be prohibitive. He is willing to accept some physical damage to himself and, if in a group, accept some casualties as a cost of doing business. Heartwarming fellow, isn't he?"

Rauch spent his life in pursuit of human predators and knows them well.

If predators had our values, they wouldn't be lying in wait to rape, to rob, or to kill. As Gavin de Becker has pointed out, it is a huge fallacy to think that people who perpetrate violent crime are those among us who just suddenly snap. Despite what you may have read or seen on television, violent criminals are not "just like us." People who have made a career of violent crime perpetrate the majority of violent crime. When we look at the criminals we might encounter on the trail, in a national park, or elsewhere in the backcountry, we overwhelmingly see a hardened criminal, not an everyday Joe or Jane about to snap.

Escalation

Andrew Branca's decision tree assumes that we ourselves do nothing to escalate the situation. Self-defense law, as well as morality, implores that we not escalate force. How do we escalate a situation? Let's go back to my parrots, Ripley and Cleo, for a few pointers. Parrots are tough; recent research of fossil records indicates that the parrots we recognize today were among the few animals to survive the theorized asteroid impact that ended the rule of the dinosaurs. So parrots have had plenty of time to refine their own rulebook, as parrot owners have painfully learned. Parrots always respond to aggression with aggression. Think about that for a minute—there's no way to de-escalate an aggressive situation with more aggression. And people, I believe, respond pretty much like parrots. Aggression is additive. Let's go back to that self-defense strategy we discussed earlier from attorney Andrew Branca:

1. Avoid
2. Placate
3. Non-Lethal Options
4. Retreat
5. Presentation
6. Engage

I consider retreat to be higher up on the strategy scale, because retreat is always preferable to a full-blown violent encounter. In fact, my decision tree, in reality, looks more like this:

1. Avoid
2. Placate/Retreat
3. Non-Lethal Options/Retreat
4. Presentation/Retreat
5. Engage/Retreat

In short, I'll take the retreat option whenever it appears —if it won't put me at greater risk. That caveat is very important. Once a violent encounter is under way, when I'm in Condition Black, my mindset has shifted to neutralizing the threat in the most beneficial manner. Attempting to retreat always has the potential to place me in greater risk. For example, I may spot an avenue of retreat, but it juts down a steep, rocky bank with lots of loose shale; should I stumble, which is certainly likely, I'll be in serious trouble, maybe injured, and unable to protect myself in any way. Retreat is always an option, but once we are in Condition Black, it is a secondary option.

Over the next few chapters, we're going to be going through our self-defense strategies, one at a time. We will discuss the pros and cons of each strategy, and will examine several examples to illuminate the concepts as much as possible. But no matter what, you won't be comfortable. That's the reality of violence.

9

Avoidance

A Trip to the Dentist

AVOIDANCE OCCUPIES THE PRIVILEGED SPACE of the first strategy on the self-defense decision tree we established in the previous chapter. As you're probably aware, we tend to avoid things that cause us pain or that impinge on our comfort zones. That's why we don't get up in the morning excited about a trip to the dentist. Given that we sometimes avoid things that are painful but good for us, we've developed a slightly squeamish feeling to accompany the whole concept of avoidance. The word has come to unpleasantly imply gutlessness, wimpiness, and trepidation.

Admit it... doesn't it seem, well, not fair to try and avoid something? Doesn't it seem better, more right, to face that thing head on; to address the issue; to stand up "like a man"? What appears to be happening here? That's right,

more of that sneaky mental programming that we've been
ferreting out throughout our exploration of safety tactics.
Most of us have been taught all our lives that it's better to
face an unpleasant situation than to avoid it. We've learned
that running away is a cop out, that it doesn't solve the root
of the problem. And in lots of aspects of our lives, that's the
absolute truth. However, this notion doesn't happen to carry
any truth in self-defense thinking. On the contrary, avoidance is our first, and best, line of defense.

Frankly, I used to think of this particular problem as an
exclusively male one. As Tex Ritter sang in the theme to the
great western film *High Noon*:

> *"The noonday train will bring Frank Miller.*
> *If I'm a man, I must be brave.*
> *And I must face a man who hates me*
> *Or lie a coward,*
> *A craven coward,*
> *Or lie a coward in my grave."*

That's some heavy baggage for men to deal with. Lately,
though, I have seen more and more women adopting the
"hit-it-head-on" approach. The reality is that there will be
situations where you, male or female, may be required to hit
it head on, very head on. Those situations will find you. You
will not find them. In the meantime, let's consider avoidance,
our first line of defense.

Let's remove whatever connotations we have developed
in connection with the word "avoidance" and see what it
actually means—to prevent the occurrence of something, or
to leave or depart from a situation. Now that has the ear-
marks of a tactically sound choice.

Back to the Basics

Assume you are two days out on a long weekend hike when you pass a familiar group of hikers. You passed them for the first time the day before. Both times you've passed, despite the fact that there have been cheery hellos all around, you've gotten a "ding" from the back of your head. Not a big fear message, but a solid warning. Something here is not as it seems. When one member of the other party calls out to you to come back and join them, you get a solid fear hit. Your awareness ratchets right up through Condition Yellow into Condition Red. Yet your common sense tells you absolutely nothing is wrong. What do you do?

Intuition-Awareness-Fear: A Review

As you'll recall, awareness furnishes the programming tools, the keystrokes we use to program our subconscious. Awareness also fuels our ability to receive data; we've already seen how we can use tools like the Awareness Color Code to help us become more aware and take in more information from our surroundings. Planning, the gathering of data by other than direct sensory means, also forms a part of our programming function. The more data we have on file, the more refined our awareness can become. Awareness, in turn, programs our intuition. Awareness instructs our brain to not send us any e-mail about a particular aspect of our environment, because we've already checked things out and everything lines up with our expectations.

Once our intuition understands the ground rules, it takes over as a sort of volume control for our awareness. Our intuition sends us a bulletin—"something is outside of parameters"—and, at the same time, turns the volume up on our awareness. With this working relationship in place, we've

now got the incredible ability to listen and learn from our
fear—we feel fear, and we're able to use the tool by accepting the warning and placing it aside so as to allow our mind
to function effectively.

Now we'll construct a decision matrix for the above situation on the trail. Remember, heavy e-mail from the back
of your head flows into your conscious mind, and one member of the other hiking party continues to call you to come
back and join them. Let's assume you're alone. Your options
include:

- Go back and join them. Maybe they're all real party
  animals.
- Ignore them and continue at your hiking pace.
- Speed up and put some distance between you and them.
  Chicken! Chicken! (Gotcha for a second there didn't I?
  See how much strength that paradigm carries?)

What should you do? Let me tell you what I would do
and, indeed, have done in a similar situation: Acknowledge
their call with a wave and a smile, as if I hadn't quite heard
what they had said but had assumed it was a friendly greet-
ing. Then speed up and put as much distance as I could
between them and me. A single person can move faster than
a group, especially when the single person's initiative drives
the movement.

Running the Distance

Here's one of my patented sweeping generalizations:
Distance is good. More distance is better. And running deliv-
ers the best way to achieve distance. When I was a kid grow-
ing up in Memphis, Tennessee, my grandfather owned a
neighborhood drugstore in an area that perched on the edge

of the long, slippery slope that ended in slum status. It was the late 1950s and early 1960s. The burger joint down the street didn't even display the "Golden Arches." For years, my grandfather employed the same deliveryman, a young black man named Rozelle. For all his polite habits at work in the drugstore, Rozelle was a legend among the flashy young rebels and the older toughs in the neighborhood, who couldn't quite find their way home from places like Iwo Jima and Normandy. Rozelle was a street warrior who carried a straight razor and was, it was whispered, a life-taker.

I didn't realize it at the time, but if you want to maintain a drugstore in a war zone, you must become tougher than the circling sharks. The relationship between my grandfather and Rozelle secured my grandfather's drugstore as an island of relative safety for years. Heading into a teenaged testosterone world, I once asked Rozelle about fighting, about being a man. The street warrior just laughed at me. "You get a chance to run," he said, "you take it. That's how it really is."

I couldn't reconcile the words I was hearing from Rozelle with this warrior's reputation. Guys from the war, guys with hollow, dead eyes, always spoke to Rozelle with respect. I tried to imagine this tough guy running away from a fight. In a kid's mind, it just didn't compute. It took years for me to understand his basic truth, learned the hard way: Bravery is characterized not by machismo, but by avoiding the situation when at all possible, because no fights are fair.

The Myth of a Fair Fight

Let me throw out yet another sweeping and scary generalization: Every potentially violent situation is a matter of life or death. Act accordingly. Click back to the 24-hour animal channel and our pals Ms. Lion and Mr. Wildebeest. Do you think that Mr. Wildebeest ever thinks to himself, "Well, she really doesn't look that hungry; maybe we're just going to have a tussle"? Every violent encounter between lion and wildebeest determines who will be dinner and who will not, and neither the diner nor the dinner has any illusions about that.

Humans on the other hand, having highly evolved brains and all, possess the apparently unique ability to convince ourselves of alternative realities. We think: "He's not really going to hurt me; he just wants my PowerBars. I can expect some minor pushing and shoving; it won't be a real fight. As long as I agree to everything, I won't encounter serious danger." Rarely will such conflicts be so pleasant, so don't count on it.

Even if we have trained extensively in some sort of self-defense exercise, we tend to underestimate violent encounters for what they can develop into. Over the years, I've spent a lot of time in martial arts dojos. Often I'd get caught in a round of what-ifs. I'd usually get the what-ifs from a newly minted black belt who wanted to explain to me that he or she was indeed someone to be reckoned with. The conversation would normally proceed thusly: "What if you're in a bar, and a guy comes up and calls you a (*fill in the blank*)? What I'd do is (*grab, twist, snatch*) his (*arm, nose, private parts*) and (*throw, drag, kick*) him right out the door! What would you do?"

I always answered the same way: "I'd get up and leave the bar."

This usually guarantees a moment of silence, followed by, "But what if he spits on your boots and says your shirt looked like a beach towel with barf on it (or something along those lines). Then what would you do?"

"Well, gee, I'd still get up and leave."

Keeping in mind that every potential confrontation is a matter of life or death, does it seem wise to have a confrontation over my poor choice in shirts (or drinking establishments)? Obviously it does not. First and foremost, choose avoidance. Because if you choose violence someone gets eaten, and that someone will likely be you.

Moving from Strategic to Tactical Thinking

If you're on the trail, and you go past someone who causes your intuition to "ding," what should you do? Let's take it one step at a time:

1. You get an e-mail from the back of your head; something doesn't seem right about the two guys who just shot past you on mountain bikes. They were going too fast for you to consciously take note, but your intuition gives you a loud and clear "ding!"

2. Immediately, you ratchet up your awareness from Condition Green to Condition Yellow. Mentally, you ask, "Does a threat exist, and if so, where? What does my environment communicate to me right now?"

3. Your conscious thinking shifts gears from strategic to tactical.

Everything we've talked about so far is characteristic of strategic thinking—all our planning, all our information gathering, and all our what-ifs are designed to give us a broad mental framework for our trip. Through our strategic thinking, we've built a functioning model of our trip, which has allowed us to play out a few scenarios in our head—for example, what if it rains or snows—and refine our plans. The last part of our strategic plan dictates that, in the case of a real situation, we'll update out strategy with real-time, tactical information and take action accordingly.

I am not necessarily in Condition Red here; I have not necessarily identified a specific threat. I would always rather, however, err on the side of caution. Therefore, my action plan might be to kill some time in another location away from the bikers in the hopes that the problems that prompted a "ding" will move on. Or I might hang back on the trail until I see a few other hikers going the same way, and then head out just ahead or behind them. As we've discussed, herds provide more safety than roughing it alone. If the "ding" I got was more urgent, I might even tell the other hikers that I was just passed by a couple of "hinky" guys, and would they mind if I tagged along with them? I then become the scout zebra that's warned the whole herd. Now several pairs of eyes watch out, and the herd is wary. If I'm really spooked, I'll turn around and go back down the trail. If I have the chance, I will retreat!

Standing Your Ground?

A couple of years back, I did some climbing in Joshua Tree National Park in southeastern California. It was getting late, and I was headed back to camp when I saw a truly strange confrontation. Joshua Tree is close enough to Los Angeles that, occasionally, some urban sludge finds its way into that wonderful desert. In this case, a couple of carloads of gang kids, dressed in full gang colors, had set up boom boxes and built roaring bonfires, which they attended rambunctiously, drinks in hand. Across the campsite sat an elderly couple in a small camper, cooking on a propane stove. The couple looked as if they had been sentenced to camp there, and appeared grim but determined.

Did that couple have every right in the world to camp in that particular spot? Absolutely. Is it unfortunate that good people should be scared to exercise their rights and have their enjoyment of the outdoors ruined? Totally. Is it also true that a dozen drunk gang members could make for a truly world-class disaster of an evening? No question.

Unfortunately, this couple had failed to complete an accurate risk assessment and had coupled that failure with a dose of the "if I'm a man, I must be brave" paradigm. First, they probably didn't fully understand the risks of spending the night next to a couple of carloads of drunken gang members. I would define this situation as a potentially lethal risk (not to hammer on gangs in particular; liquor is always an escalating factor, regardless of the make-up of the group of drinkers).

Second, our elderly couple made a decision to stand their ground, perhaps to prove the point that the outdoors belongs to us all. I agree with the sentiment; however, the tactics leave something to be desired. I know that the lion will surely lay down with the lamb, that Democrats will one day wed Republicans, and that the meek shall inherit the earth. But, as the punch line to the old joke goes, that's not the way to bet.

I have found through my travels of the backcountry that times arise when you are obligated—morally, legally, and ethically—to stand your ground. But I believe that if we are to be victorious in our endeavors, we need to understand the difference between courage and ego. Every potential confrontation is not *High Noon* with the lone marshal, Gary Cooper, facing men committed to killing him. But *High Noon* is out there. We don't need to go looking for it. As the great Bruce Lee once wrote, "Do not run away; let go. Do not seek, for it will come when least expected."

A philosophy of avoidance has nothing to do with the degree to which you prepare for a confrontation. The next several chapters will take you a little farther along the lines of preparation. I hope that after reading this book, you take more positive steps to live strategically and be ready for whatever life may throw at you, whether it's on the trail or in your office. However, if you only take one thing away from this book, please let it be to preserve the option of avoidance as your first and best option.

10

Retreat

Distance is Good

WE'VE TALKED AT LENGTH NOW about using the incredible mechanisms in our head to keep us out of trouble. We always have some sort of programming function available to us, whether it's intuition or awareness or fear. Programming also applies to our *reactions* to our warning system. Now that you're used to listening to your head, let me point out the first of our programmed responses: Distance is good. We are at maximum risk when a person is at an arms-length distance or less from us. Distance is our friend, and we want to hammer that into our heads.

Stated another way, the farther a threat is from you, the less of a threat it actually is. However, we have come to underestimate how far from an assailant we need to settle ourselves to remain safe. I once participated in a self-defense drill that most cops attend these days aimed at teaching officers how quickly an assailant with a knife can close on an armed person and inflict potentially lethal damage. Massad Ayoob, director of the Lethal Force Institute (LFI) in Concord, New Hampshire, originally developed the drill. LFI strives to dispel a lot of the myths around self-defense, and presents as its basic offering a grueling 40-hour course on the realities of self-defense. This knife drill particularly struck me as one of the most paradigm-shattering parts of the course. The instructor had given a rubber knife to one of the students and had then had him stand seven yards (21 feet) away from a second student. When my turn came, those seven yards appeared to stretch into a fairly long distance. I remember standing there, looking at this guy across the parking lot with a rubber knife, thinking, "He is in a different time zone. Threat? Yeah, sure." The simple drill commenced when the instructor triggered a timer and the guy with the rubber knife attacked.

It will most likely surprise you to discover that only 1.5 seconds elapsed during the attack, from the time the buzzer sounded until the rubber knife smacked into my chest, directly over my heart. Take a look at the room you occupy right now. Get up and pace the distance across the room. My hotel room where I work this evening spans about 14 feet across, which equates to less than a second of crossing time for a determined assailant.

Exit Stage Whatever!

Our first and most basic response to the intuition e-mail must be avoidance. The second strategy directs us to, if given the choice, exit stage right (or left or front or back—whichever is available). Given my druthers, I will almost always attempt to retreat from a situation. I hate to keep throwing in all these hedge words like "almost," but each potential situation is distinctive. I can tell you my strategic framework, but I can't guarantee that the next situation will absolutely lend itself to retreat. Switching to tactical thinking the second you encounter a violent situation in the real world is thus critical to selecting the best strategy. Retreat remains, however, always in the front of my mind.

Among the reasons we've been focusing on intuition, awareness, and fear lies the fact that these three tools can buy us time. We get a "ding" from our intuition; we ratchet up our awareness; we may well get an additional bulletin from fear . . . we've just bought some time. Instead of walking smack into a situation, we've received an early warning. That extra time allows us to avoid the situation; if we can't avoid, we'll retreat.

I must now point out the distinction between avoidance and retreat in this context. I generally think of avoidance as something that happens very early on in the process, propelled by either my awareness of a potential situation or by one of those intuition e-mails. Retreat, on the other hand, implies that I have crossed some invisible line into a situation: for example, as we discussed in the previous chapter, having a gang set up a rowdy camp next to my serene nest of sleeping bags and propane stoves. Deciding whether you're avoiding or retreating is not something to which you need to allocate precious mental resources; suffice to say that both strategies fall into the category of pre-event management.

Mysterious Asian Wisdom

It's worth taking a moment to note what we're trying to accomplish here in pre-event management. Most of you who have attended business school in the past ten years will remember Sun Tzu's *The Art of War*, a slim book of strategy written by a Chinese general more than 25 centuries ago. I like Sun Tzu, and all those business school professors like the old boy as well, because he cuts through the fog right to the heart of conflict. He asks, what are we doing here, and what is the best way to accomplish our goals?

In my favorite translation of *The Art of War*, edited by novelist James Clavell of *Shogun* and *Tai-Pan* fame, Clavell notes that many of our military fiascoes could have been avoided had our military leaders read and followed the teachings of this volume. On tactics, Sun Tzu wrote, "True excellence is to plan secretly, to move surreptitiously, to foil the enemy's intentions and balk his schemes, so that at last the day may be won without shedding a drop of blood." Think about that: "Foil the enemy's intentions and balk his schemes." Now think about this: nothing can happen to me if I'm not there. Avoidance and retreat inherently foil the enemy's intentions and balk his schemes.

If I want a chance to avoid or retreat I must be aware of the situation. We need to be in Condition Green with relaxed awareness any time we are out of the house: taking in everything going on around us; ready to read, then avoid, or retreat from, any developing situation. Years back, in my tenure as a journalist, I spent time at some of the nation's largest urban riots. The one thing that really struck me (aside from a few rocks, tear gas, and one really painful police baton) was how many citizens simply wandered into the riot, blissfully unaware of the madness surrounding them. It utterly amazed me—the scenery included sirens, flashing lights, clouds of drifting gas, groups of people chased hither and yon by riot-clad police, assorted small fires, all manner of pandemonium. And in wanders a woman sharply dressed in a suit holding a briefcase, looking as if she had just woken up on an alien planet.

You must first pay attention; then you must listen to the e-mail from the back of your head. Intuition will tell you when something in your immediate environment doesn't add up. Let your brain work, that superbly tuned information-gathering device. You don't have the time or the RAM to study every piece of incoming data about your environment. But your subconscious does, and when it detects an anomaly—if you've been following my recommendations and listening—it lets you know.

Programming Distance

We do, in essence, what we're programmed to do. Or, more accurately, what we program ourselves to do. If you've ever taken white-water kayak lessons, you've learned that you can't be a serious kayaker if you don't learn something called an Eskimo roll. Basically, an Eskimo roll provides a way to right the kayak after it's turned over in the water. It requires a little snap of the hip coupled with a strategic push of the oar, all performed while submerged upside down (and thus, underwater) in the kayak. Boy, does that sound easy! Well, it isn't. It's a little like learning to juggle while driving your car and holding your breath. Once you have it down, however, it becomes more and more like driving a car—an automatic reflex. Boat turns over; you pop it right back up. You have programmed a response, the Eskimo roll, to a specific stimulus, being upside down in white water.

We want to program in the response "Distance is good" in the same way, so that creating distance becomes a second-nature response, accompanying avoidance and retreat as your first two steps in the self-defense strategy. We've been talking about distance in the macro sense—leave the area. But distance is also important in the micro sense—when you're already close to someone, and that someone is not someone to whom you want to be close. As I stated above: We are at maximum risk when a person is at an arms-length distance or less from us.

Personally Spaced Out

Often, in self-defense classes, people learn not let anyone inside their "personal space." The definition of personal space that suits our purposes here describes this area as a circle centered on the body that measures six feet in diameter. This typically is accurate, unless of course we live in New York City, where our personal space is defined as "touching."

The concept of personal space is an *urban* concept; when we visit the backcountry, we have the luxury of extending our personal space. Usually, I enjoy people I meet on the trail. I do, however, trust my intuition and awareness. Put in a pessimistic way, you might say that I make snap judgements about people, sometimes from a distance. And then I act on those snap judgements. If something in my immediate environment causes me to shift my awareness from Condition Green to Condition Yellow, or to get a "ding" from the back of my head, I will put as much distance as I can between me and whatever or whomever causes me to be cautious.

Let's go back to the scenario in the previous chapter— you are alone and you've passed a group of people that give you a solid fear "ding." One of them yells for you to join them. Remember I suggested that I would wave and speed up. I would create distance.

RULES FOR PERSONAL SPACE

Let's expand this into some general rules:

1. *When someone says, "Come here," don't.* If you are in Condition Yellow, do not close with another person or group of people. Keep your distance. In general, I don't think it's a good idea to respond to a verbal command from anyone you don't know while out on the trail, unless it's clearly an emergency situation. "Come here," "Slow down," and "Stop" are generally best dealt with by a friendly wave. Maybe point to your ear as if you can't hear. Then put some distance between you and whoever is talking.

2. *In Condition Yellow, do not let anyone close with you.* This is the converse of our first point. I think of this point as sort of a Charlie Chaplin dance step—you take a step toward me; I take a step back.

3. *Slowing down is often more effective than speeding up.* Unless you've got your cell phone and can reach the Psychic Friends Network, you don't know who's on the trail in front of you. But you do know who's on the trail behind you. As I've mentioned, my partner and I tend to be really fast hikers; part of the fun of being outdoors is the exercise aspect. However, on more than one occasion, we've slowed down and let ourselves fall among (or directly behind) a larger group of hikers.

4. *Herds can be good things.* You'll notice I haven't said much about hiking by yourself. Hiking alone is a personal choice. I've spent many happy hours alone in the wilderness. Nevertheless, please understand that hiking alone merits more attention in your risk assessment, especially if you're a woman. If you're on a popular trail

or in a heavily populated recreational area, joining a herd, even briefly, is a solid safety tactic. I've used it many times.

5. *A solid object between thee and me makes me harder to get to.* Trees and boulders are definitely solid objects. If I can step in such a way that a large impediment stands between whatever has bumped me into Condition Yellow, I'll always do so. It doesn't cost me anything, and the other person merely considers me cautious or crazy—a perception that suits me fine. Your outdoor gear will work as a solid object too. For example, during a heated discussion over trail access recently, my mountain bike was always between the other person and me.

Let's recap here before we press on. Retreat remains a perpetual option throughout your self-defense strategy, but is easier to accomplish earlier in the process; we might think of an early retreat as a late avoidance. Integral to this early escape is paying attention to your awareness and trusting in your intuition. If you feel like the situation is hinky, *bail*, because from here on out, the situations get tougher to deal with.

11

Placate

The Art of Placation

AS ANYONE WHO HAS EVER YELLED at her little sister or talked back to parents or gotten into a vicious argument with a significant other knows, words are weapons. Contrary to the playground taunt, while sticks and stones will break your bones, words can *indeed* hurt you—they can cut to the quick. For our purposes, in fact, words can act as defensive weapons, transforming into another tool for our self-defense arsenal. Words can placate.

I would like to tell you that you can resolve every potentially violent situation with placation and a good rap; as science-fiction writer Isaac Asimov once wrote in his Foundation series, "Violence is the last resort of the incompetent." Unfortunately, violent and dangerous incompetents do lurk out there, and they have to be dealt with in some fashion. I have talked my way out of several potentially dangerous situations with such individuals, and have been happy with those results. Do not have the illusion, however, that words will *always* work. Nothing always works; however, the more tools we have in our arsenal, the more likely we are to find *something* that works. At this point, we have tried avoidance and we have attempted to retreat; unfortunately, these two strategies either have not been available or were not effective for whatever reason. Therefore, we now move up the decision tree to placation.

Words need to be part of our self-defense strategy in order to satisfy two goals: to soothe and calm (otherwise known as placation) and to buy time. These goals are not necessarily distinct; in fact, they tend to occur simultaneously. During this process of stalling, we can evaluate alternatives and formulate further tactical plans.

Let's begin our consideration of this self-defense strategy by examining placation from the inside out: What placates you? When you're really pissed off and you feel yourself winding up like the mainspring of a cheap mechanical clock, what actions by a friend, a spouse, or a complete stranger cause you to start winding down?

Personally, when the object of my anger or stress escalation doesn't play along, I calm considerably. If I perceive that the other person's body language and verbal clues signal to me that I have nothing to gain, I lose momentum and my tendency toward violence decreases.

Body Language

Showing an assailant that you're not participating in his or her escalation of force can be accomplished in a variety of ways. First, you can engage in strategic physical actions that convey your mental intentions through body language. If I am a male and I want to placate someone, I will attempt to send non-threatening, maybe even submissive, signals to the person who's winding up. I might squat on my haunches, thereby placing myself lower than my assailant and giving him the impression that I do not threaten him. Or I might turn my palms out in the universal expression of, "I hold no weapons; therefore, I am not a threat." I do not cross my arms in front of my chest; I do not step forward; I do not consciously or unconsciously assume a fighting stance of any kind (usually constituted by quartering the body toward the other person, allowing a punch or kick to be easily and quickly thrown).

Notice that I tailored these instructions for men. I believe the situation differs dramatically in terms of body language for a woman. Think about the environment that a female inhabits on a trail, in a foreign country, or anywhere in the backcountry. If she has entered a situation that has delivered an intuitive "ding," and has perhaps felt a rush of fear, in all probability, the source of that "ding" will appear in the form of one or more men. Therefore, she should not send any signal that intends to mean or might be interpreted to mean, "I am helpless and therefore am less of a threat." For women, I believe that the risks in such a signal far, far outweigh the potential gain. Already at a disadvantage in terms of weight, reach (by arms and legs), and probably, unless you're a professional adventure racer, strength, the average woman does not need to send any submissive signals.

For women, I'd suggest sending either mixed signals or a clear signal of strength. A mixed signal might comprise, for example, taking a step back and quartering your body to the potential threat, yet continuing to show your open palms. This communicates, "I retreat, and I offer no threat, but I am prepared to fight." A clear signal of strength might involve not stepping back and facing the potential threat face on—"I do not feel the need to retreat, and I am prepared to fight."

For both men and women, don't cross your hands in front of your body. This action sends a message of fear and also makes it more difficult for you to bring your arms into play should you need them. I also advocate ambiguous moves, for example, placing my dominant hand quickly into a coat pocket or hastily unzipping a fanny pack (which I do wear in front). Remember that backcountry criminals look for targets of opportunity. The hint that you might be armed may be enough to dissuade the casual criminal.

Verbal Combat

Sooner or later, you're going to have to say something. But before we get into the best way to talk yourself *out* of trouble, let's look at some of the things assailants might use to lure you *into* trouble. A few years back, I got an interesting telephone call. Would I, the caller asked, be interested in being a psychotic? Well, there are those who are of the opinion that I've already achieved a state of derangement, but no one had ever called with a special telephone offer. The caller soon revealed himself as a SWAT police officer and said that he wanted to know if I would participate in a SWAT training exercise. The advantage to using civilians in cop exercises is that we civilians don't suffer from cop-think. Think back to the Robert McNamara Defense Department of the Vietnam War. A classic social problem emerged constantly from those grim days. Imagine that you assemble a bunch of white, Ivy League guys who have the same background, belong to the same clubs, have the same hobbies, are friendly with the same people, eat at the same restaurants, and are married to the same types of women. If you ask them a question such as, "Should we bomb the hell out of this little country," you get the same answer. Historically, police departments have tended to be fairly homogenous to begin with, and all the recruits always go through extensive training together, resulting in an increasingly nondiversified group. Asking outsiders to help with training provided the best way to get outside the box.

This particular SWAT team wanted to break in two new hostage negotiators. My role entailed acting psychotic for two days while the negotiators tried to talk me out of various scenarios. Rather than giving you a blow-by-blow account, suffice it to say that I "killed" the first negotiator five minutes into the first scenario because he pissed me off and I was, after all, crazy. The second negotiator lasted until the second day when, in a fit of frustration in a face-to-face session, he grabbed me by the shirt and called me a "moronic asshole." I felt really sorry for him, since he was immediately relieved of duty and required to repeat hostage negotiation training.

Now these scenarios were controlled situations with the police brass looking on. Both negotiators knew that if they didn't perform to par, they would be relieved of negotiation duty. Both knew that I had been instructed by the SWAT commander to play the role of an intransigent psychotic. Both knew that this was a game and that nobody's life was on the line. Yet both failed because I was able to verbally escalate the situation to a point where even fledgling negotiators lost their cool.

I accomplished this (other than by being born with a big mouth) through careful observation of my subjects. Initially, I shot out verbal abuse, a sort of word storm. Then I watched my baby negotiators for their reactions—a clenched jaw here, an angry expression there. While I blathered, I continuously cataloged what worked, what pushed their buttons. As we moved through the day, I began returning to what had worked, then hitting those hot buttons again and again. Slightly overweight? Hair thinning? Sharply creased jeans? All fodder for my raging psychosis. Every so often, the negotiator would inadvertently give me something new by making a verbal slip that I was able to turn around and use against him, such as when he compared me to his wife. I had a field day with that one!

I've put together this list of factors that I've found tend to contribute to escalating situations to violence:

- *Lack of continuity.* We expect people to talk sequentially: "C" follows "B" follows "A." Increasing repetition of phrases or questions grates on some primeval nerve. For example, think of Robert DeNiro as the more-than-slightly crazed Travis in *Taxi Driver*: "You talkin' to *me*? You *talkin'* to me?"

- *Sarcasm.* Someone once wrote, "Sarcasm is the death of love." Sarcasm is also the quickest way to escalate a situation. Some people (and I used to be among them) believe in sarcasm the way some people believe in Elvis and are keenly attuned to finding the best place in which to stick that barb. Sarcasm is, in essence, a carefully tailored personal insult.

- *Challenge.* An obvious verbal challenge ups the ante. If you intentionally try to escalate a situation, you should present challenges later on in the escalation cycle; my negotiators had watched for challenges early on, but as the exercises lengthened, they dropped their guards and I was able to get a more satisfying response.

- *Whining.* I describe whining as the verbal equivalent of fingernails on a chalkboard. Any parents out there will agree with a hearty "Amen!" on this point.
- *Mood swings.* While not precisely verbal, mood swings on your part serve to rattle the other party, which make the other party susceptible to the other escalating factors.
- *Fatigue.* The longer a situation drags on, the more nerves—and defenses against verbal escalation—fray on both sides. The longer a situation drags on, the more likely it will escalate.

Interestingly enough, professional interviewers use many of these verbal escalation factors to extract information from recruits. As the interviewer of a tough, media-wise subject, I might use any one (or several) of these techniques to ratchet up the anxiety level of the interviewee, hoping to get a solid response from him or her. Observational awareness supplies the key to interviewing in exactly the same way as it supplies the key to ruining a couple of hostage negotiators' day. We all telegraph our feelings, some people more than others.

We do this every day, in every conceivable situation. We read people, and respond accordingly. Now that we have learned the ways in which an assailant might escalate force, we can watch for these signals and avoid getting sucked in by them. If we are aware—say in Condition Red, keenly focused on a specific threat—we can factor that incoming *tactical* information into what we say to our assailant.

Blubbering Forebrains

As you'll recall, our biggest danger in a high-fear situation is that the thinking part of our brain wants to shut down, a victim of our "flee-or-fight" software. Yes, our physical responses need to happen as fast as lightning while our thoughts get routed through our lizard brain. However, this doesn't mean that our reasoning-self gets to take a short holiday. We need to operate and think simultaneously. We need to immediately take tactical actions based on our strategic plan and our current environment, and we also need to analyze incoming information and prepare to take advantage of opportunities.

We can't do all that if our forebrain sits there blubbering. Firstly, if we either graze on the cusp of, or actually encounter, a potentially violent situation, we're going to get some solid fear hits. As we've discussed, we need to respond by acknowledging our fear and then setting it aside so we can get out of harm's way. Secondly, we need to plug the real-time tactical information into our strategic plan. Thirdly, we need to look for opportunities to either get out of the situation or buy time to improve our tactical position. Finally, we need to evaluate alternatives at some level. These activities will overlap quite a bit.

The Doped-Up-Dog Debacle

Let me give you an example of how I've noted the factors of escalation used by a threatening assailant, processed all of the above cognitive steps (despite the presence of a challenged mental position resulting from fear), and successfully placated the assailant. One night I was foraging around in my car at a trailhead for some aspirin and a box of dog biscuits for my dog back at the campsite. The aspirin was for a fierce headache; the Milk Bones were an afterthought. Having the two items in hand, I had closed the door and turned to head back to camp when another car pulled up alongside mine. The passenger climbed out and started around the front of his car toward me. Along the way, he pulled out a small knife; then he stopped.

I retraced the few feet back to my car door, set the aspirin on the hood of the car, and gestured with the dog biscuits. "I gotta get back to camp," I said to my mugger, trying to look very inner-city. "My dog's a hype, and he's climbing the walls."

The guy looked at me as if I'd just beamed in from Jupiter. "Your dog's a junkie?" he asked, not moving.

"Yep," I said, picking up the aspirin bottle. "I'm doing what I can for him, but he's coming down hard."

"Like, a real junkie?" he still didn't move.

I, on the other hand, had proceeded to unlock the door, open it, and then step behind it. I now had the front of my car and the car door between the man with the knife and me. The driver of the other car had both hands on the wheel, where I could clearly see them. I just kept right on with my rap, spinning a sad tale about my poor dog.

By the time my mugger had started to laugh, I was in the car with the door closed, the key in the ignition, and the dog biscuits and aspirin on the hood. The man's penknife seemed unlikely to break auto glass, and I could still see the driver's hands. I started the car.

"Get out of here," my mugger said. "You're one crazy white boy. A junkie dog! Can you believe it!"

Here's the kicker—I had a legally licensed gun on my person. This point aside, at no point in the encounter did I lose control of the situation. At no point did I allow my mugger to gain a direct line to my person; I always kept *something*—the dog biscuits, the car hood, the car door—between him and me. However, had I lost sight of the driver's hands, or had the driver attempted to get out of the car, I would have drawn my weapon, and the situation would have escalated into a whole different realm. Had my mugger not stopped moving when I started my dog story, the situation also would have been different. I did not draw my weapon because I saw an opportunity to de-escalate the situation when my mugger responded to my silly tale. Given my druthers, I'll tell a stupid story and get the heck out of Dodge, even if my attacker is armed, rather than escalate force by presenting a weapon of my own, however justified that force might seem.

Dangers of the Trailhead

The example above presents an opportunity to describe a few practical tips and general rules for trailheads. I put these together because the point on your hike when you are at the greatest risk is when you are at the parking lot at the trailhead. Like my potential mugger, snatch-and-grab criminals are relatively lazy. They have little or no desire to hike five hours up the trail to snatch your daypack, wallet, and fleece jacket. Better to snatch that stuff at the trailhead and maybe get the car as a bonus. Because you're excited to get on the trail—you're anticipating the physical challenges and the beautiful vistas you'll experience, and you're unloading your equipment and so on—you may not be as attentive as you should be. That makes you an excellent target for a predator.

So before we get back to talking your way out of situations, let me give you a quick set of rules for trailheads:

SAFETY RULES FOR TRAILHEADS

1. *If it looks suspicious, leave.* For example, a sedan with the motor running and four silhouettes inside parked at

a trailhead just before dawn is suspicious. A thick cloud of marijuana smoke classifies as suspicious. Anything your intuition defines as "suspicious" is suspicious; act on that intuition. Go back into town and have breakfast. Try an alternate trailhead. Remember how you thought that elderly couple camped out by Los Angeles gang members in an earlier chapter were stupid? Don't make the same mistake.

2. *Be efficient in getting on the trail.* I've seen couples who managed to spread enough gear to outfit an entire REI store around a trailhead parking lot. This might resemble a rummage sale to snatch-and-grab artists. Pack at home.

3. *Be friendly with, but wary of, fellow hikers.* I'm not advocating becoming a lonely and cold person; in fact, I tend to exercise extreme friendliness with those out to enjoy the wilderness as I am. However, I am generally wary of people who want to be my new best friend, who offer to help me sort and carry my gear, who appear out of place or inappropriately dressed (what's with them slippery city shoes, anyway?), or who cause the back of my head to send me an e-mail. What do you do if you get a strong "ding?" See Rule 1.

4. *Leave the car open until you're ready to hit the trail.* Always nice to have that substantial steel exit pod available. By telling the story about my junkie dog, I had intended to buy time enough to open and get into my car. Cars are relatively sturdy metal boxes. The glass is amazingly strong (I know because I've pounded on the glass of junk cars just to see how hard it was to shatter) and the locks provide another piece of strong protection. You are armored in your car. And you can *drive away*! As an

added bonus, you are now behind the wheel of a multi-thousand-pound lethal weapon. Even if the other party has a gun, they will have difficulty hitting a moving target. So as a matter of habit, I usually leave the car door open until the last minute, which also keeps me from locking my keys in the car.

5. *Pack the car keys last, and always place them in the same accessible location.* Again, the car is your escape pod; make it as easy as possible to use that pod. I have friends who arrive at the trailhead, open the rear door of the SUV, immediately lock both front doors, and throw the keys into a gigantic expedition backpack, where they are promptly buried in a nest of old PowerBars. Avoid this syndrome by designating a small pocket for car keys and consistently packing them in that pocket.

How to Talk Your Way Out of Almost Anything

Now that I've given you some pointers on how to stay safe at the trailhead, I'll present some equally practical suggestions for how to talk yourself out of trouble: As always, don't assume that the strategy you pick—in this case, placation—will work. Keep in mind that you have a whole self-defense strategy, of which talking is only a part. When you choose placation, follow the guidelines below.

- *Don't engage the other party in a dialog.* Your intent here is to de-escalate and buy time. Keep your answers short. Another reason to avoid complex dialog is that you're going to need your mind for other, more important purposes. I tend to agree with people who call me names—whatever you call me, I'll say, "You're right; I'm a whatever."
- *Watch your tone of voice.* Some negotiators suggest that

you match your tone of voice to the other party's tone of voice. Conversely, I believe that your tone of voice should be flat and devoid of emotional content. Especially avoid a sarcastic or challenging tone, as the other party will listen to you as closely as you listen to them.

- *Try to project control and a lack of fear*, even if you've only barely managed to acknowledge your fear and set it aside. Predators always recognize prey. The other party is not interested in engaging you in a spirited debate. He or she is, rather, running a risk-versus-reward analysis. Anything you can do to add to the "risk" side of that analysis will benefit you. The exhibition of control and of a lack of fear sets off a warning bell in some predators' minds. They wonder: Are you not afraid because you're stupid, or are you not afraid because the Denver Broncos football team is one minute behind you on the trail and you have a hand grenade in your fanny pack? You need to establish a reasonable doubt in the predator's mind that you are fit to be eaten. Mixed signals, as I discussed earlier, are especially useful in such situations. I might say how scared I am, but my body language might not reflect fear. This will hopefully create a reasonable doubt in my potential assailant's mind like this one, "*Perhaps he is not what I think he is . . . do I want to take that chance?*"

- *Further the ambiguity by creating a relationship and a feeling of empathy with the assailant.* People respond better to any question or tense verbal situation if they perceive that there is a relationship with the other person; interestingly enough, it doesn't seem to matter whether it is a positive or a negative relationship. It's therefore in your best interest to establish some sort of relationship as quickly as possible.

One of the main tools I use to establish a relationship with a predator comes from the movies. As you probably already know, movies are actually the result of a series of still photographs projected in rapid sequence. Our brain looks at those stills, fills in the missing parts, and informs us that the action is taking place continuously.

Movie guys call this "persistence of vision." The folks who make television commercials seized on this little bit of information in the 1960s and expanded on the theme. Suppose, they reasoned, huge chunks of the narrative were removed; how much was the brain prepared to fill in? They discovered that, after the presentation of 30 seconds of images for Acme Ketchup, for example, the average person's brain derives from the commercial that Acme Ketchup is responsible for the rise of western civilization.

In short, one of our brain's major roles is to fill in the blanks. Knowing that, I throw out chunks of incomplete thoughts that, with the blanks filled in by our opposing party, create a reasonable doubt in his or her mind. An actual dialog might progress as follows:

"You scared, asshole?"

"Yes, very," I reply, with as flat a monotone as I can muster. I try to remove any hint of emotion from my face.

The other party pauses for a moment. They have observed the right verbal answer with the wrong emotional cue. There are blanks here, and blanks must be filled in. The attacker might fill this blank with something like, "The little asshole has an ace up his sleeve . . . " Then the other party might say, "You should be scared, asshole, 'cause I can really &#!% you up."

"What?" as blank as I can be. "What?"

"I said, you son of a bitch, that . . . " And so forth.

But the opposing party might by now have taken a step back, which tells me the risk-versus-reward equation has shifted slightly in my favor. I take a step back, then a long one to the side. He has done nothing but keep telling me how afraid I should be.

The risk-versus-reward analysis remains more in my favor if the other party is talking, especially cursing and threatening me. The more a person questions my ancestry and tells me how much trouble I'm in, the more I think that person actually escalates his or her own situation as they essentially pump themselves up to take action. Since they have not reached a trigger point for violent action, I have an opportunity to try and de-escalate the situation.

Watch the other party's nonverbal response to whatever you say, and stick with what works. For instance, If I make short, noncommittal responses and then observe that the other party's breathing has gotten faster and faster and that a flush has come to his or her cheeks, I'm going to shut up! I am doing more harm than good. If, on the other hand, my mugger comes to a halt to listen to my story about a doggie doper, I'm going to keep right on talking—and planning.

The Next Step

If you successfully de-escalate the situation with placation, the potential for violence *has not* disappeared. Get the hell out of there! Find a group going back to the trailhead; tell them what just happened and that you need a ranger. Then stay with them. If you don't spot any groups, head toward the closest phone, even if it's in your car at the trailhead. In technical diving, when one piece of equipment—no matter how small—fails, the dive gets called. Similarly, a potentially violent encounter on the trail is grounds for bagging the trip for three reasons:

1. The other party has not disappeared and may, after considerable thought, alcohol, or drugs, not find your de-escalation all that enchanting.

2. After the event, you're going to suffer a massive adrenaline meltdown. The machine has been running wide open, and you're going to pay a physical cost for that level of concentration. A worst-case situation is a second encounter while you're still physically drained from the first.

3. You have an obligation to notify the authorities and other people whom you might pass on the trail.

Here's the really good news—you have resolved one of the most threatening situations you'll encounter in the backcountry by this point. You have avoided, you have retreated, or you have successfully talked your way out of a tight situation. Congratulations! You have done well.

Now we will cross a line in our self-defense strategy that resembles the ancient crossing of the Rubicon by Caesar in 49 BC. For those of you who, like me, slept through high school history class, long ago Caesar led his armies across the Rubicon River, which marked the boundary between Italy proper and Gaul, and launched a big-time civil war. Since then, we have used the phrase "crossing the Rubicon" to indicate the taking of an irrevocable step into a hazardous enterprise. And that is, indeed, what we are about to do.

12

Non-Lethal Options

When Talking Fails

WHEN YOU CROSS THE RUBICON, you move into Condition Black. As you'll recall, Condition Black awareness kicks in when you detect an environment in which a violent situation quite certainly threatens your life. When you move into the world of Condition Black, the primal laws of the universe become much more apparent. Driven by the chemical factories in your body, time itself seems to decelerate. You feel as if you move as slowly as a prehistoric insect once did in amber. Your predator senses have gone into full operation. Your vision and hearing has tunneled to allow you to more effectively focus on the threat. Your extremities may shake a little as your body reroutes the blood supply to prepare you to flee or fight. The great organic chemical factory stands by with painkillers and strength enhancers. You are truly a child of the ancient killer apes; on some genetic level, your body remembers fights to the death. You are ready.

No saber-toothed tigers, dire wolves, or close cousins with rock-tipped spears and clubs of bone roam our wilderness. We now face different predators that are no less dangerous. We carry the baggage of our collective evolution. Once we've crossed our Rubicon, we will need all the legacies of our ancient past. We will also need our ultimate weapons, our brains, if we are going to prevail.

Non-Lethal Options

At this point on your self-defense decision tree, you will employ non-lethal options. Even though you will engage in violent fighting of some kind, the goal is still to preserve the life of your opponent. Non-lethal options for attack come in many forms, and I will attempt to expose you to some of them.

There is one inescapable truth here—I can't teach you how to fight. No book can. Any book that makes this claim tells you a dangerous lie. The mastery of defensive techniques, just like the mastery of the techniques for rock climbing, kayaking, or mountain biking, is rooted in repetition. Think about the most basic skill one learns in rock climbing—how to tie the figure-8 knot that connects the rope to the harness. I have tied figure-8 knots in pitch-black darkness amidst a screaming blizzard, wearing thick gloves as the thermometer plummeted to 40 degrees below. I could probably tie a figure-8 knot in my sleep. Yet I remember, after a few climbing lessons, attempting to tie that knot, trying again and again and again and getting it wrong. Getting it once, and not being able to get it again. Thousands of repetitions later my understanding extended from my mind so that, finally, my fingers understood what was required of them. From then on, I got it every time. The same repetition of tasks was demanded in my quest for mastery over the various types of martial arts in which I have trained. It's worth noting that on the very last day I trained in a dojo where I had spent many hours and many years, I performed exactly the same drills that I had learned on the first day I walked into that dojo—no magic, just practice, practice, practice.

The Seven Principles

Though I can't magically turn you into a prizefighter with just some simple instructions, I can pass on to you some tricks for programming yourself to best deal with your reactions to Condition Black, should you have the bad luck to find yourself in such a threatening situation. In 1972, a former Marine colonel named Jeff Cooper, who went on to become probably the most influential authority on police and military weapons training in the world, wrote a little 42-page pamphlet titled *Principles of Personal Defense*. Colonel Cooper chose to deal not with specific fighting tactics, but instead with the honing of our most effective weapon: our mind-set. I've probably owned a dozen copies of this pamphlet over the years; the copy I have now is brown with age. It remains, however, (along with Sun Tzu's *The Art of War*, Miyamoto Musashi's *Book of Five Rings*, Bruce Lee's *The Tao of Jeet Kune Do* and, perversely, Herbert's epic novel *Dune*) an underpinning of my own philosophy of self-defense. Cooper's seven principles have proven themselves to me again and again in the real world, and they will serve you just as well. The seven principles are:

1. Alertness
2. Decisiveness

3. Aggressiveness
4. Speed
5. Coolness
6. Ruthlessness
7. Surprise

Let's examine these principles one by one. I won't expand upon *alertness*, as I hope that, after all of our discussions regarding awareness, you have a pretty good handle on this concept by now.

Decisiveness, or total commitment to an action plan, is demanded once your feet hit the ground on the other side of the Rubicon. Unfortunately, our culture does not particularly cultivate 100-percent commitment. When you cross into Condition Black, however, you must be 100-percent committed, or you will fail.

I accomplish this decisiveness with the help of my Awareness Color Code. Mentally, I think of each step up in awareness level—from Green to Yellow to Red to Black—as a gate: I pass through a gate to get from Green to Yellow; I pass through a gate to get from Yellow to Red. Each time I pass through one of those gates, I leave behind the concerns specific to the previous condition. When I go from Condition Green to Condition Yellow, for example, I no longer ask myself, "Is something amiss?" Because I have gone to Condition Yellow, I already know something is amiss and now occupy myself with trying to figure out what. Similarly, in Condition Red, I have evaluated tactical options; when I cross over into Condition Black, I must act on an option. I commit myself to an action plan, and I abandon all the questions and uncertainties back in Condition Red.

Cooper's third principle is *aggressiveness*. Aggressiveness stems from anger, and anger stems from fear. When you cross into Condition Black you will definitely feel fear. Fear always demands a response, and in Condition Black, the response is anger. Fear drives anger; anger drives aggressiveness. Aggressiveness tells the body that it is to fight, not flee, and all that ancient software kicks in. By remembering that every potentially violent situation is a matter of life or death, you will achieve aggressiveness. Make no mistake—you fight for your life here.

The next principle is *speed*. In my business seminars, I instruct, "When in doubt, go faster." Once you are in Condition Black, speed is your best friend. Colonel Cooper states, "The perfect fight is one that is over before the loser really understands what is going on. The perfect defense is a counterattack that succeeds before the assailant discovers that he has bitten off more than he can chew." I believe that speed is even more critical for women than for men. Like it or not, men typically expect women to be submissive. Again, beware the generalization, but if you are a woman on the trail and face two men who you are certain mean you harm, their expectations open a tiny window for you. If you act quickly, you can take advantage of that window. Ralph Waldo Emerson once wrote, "When skating over thin ice, our salvation is in our speed." He was never more right than in Condition Black.

Coolness, the fifth principle of personal defense, seems to contradict the principle of raging aggressiveness. Real anger, though, is a cold, white flame that leaves your brain— your best weapon—free to function. Cool anger doesn't blind your vision. The tools you use to respond to and utilize fear as an early warning system are the same tools that have taught you how to be cool in a tight situation. Colonel Cooper says it best, "If you know that you *can* keep your head, and that you *must* keep your head, you will probably keep your head."

Ruthlessness is the sixth principle, and is a tough frame of mind to inhabit, especially for those of you who optimistically believe that inherent goodness and purity exist in all creatures. Remember that you have crossed the Rubicon. You have entered a landscape where the agreed-upon rules that govern your everyday life have been stripped away. When you cross this river, when you step through this gate, you can no longer be concerned in the least about your assailant outside of pure tactical considerations. It cannot matter to you what his or her sex is, or what the color of his or her skin is. You cannot care about his or her religion, national origin, or sexual preference. You cannot care whether your assailant had a hard childhood, was abused, lost his or her job through no fault of his or her own, suffers from a mental illness, or is just down on his or her luck. You can be concerned with one thing and one thing only—making the assailant stop immediately. If you must fight, fight hard and ruthlessly. You are not the one who has named the game here. You have done everything in your power to avoid or de-escalate the situation. If force continues to escalate despite your efforts, you must put a stop to that force entirely.

The final principle of personal defense is *surprise*. Do the unexpected. As Colonel Cooper notes, the unexpected usually consists of an instant, aggressive counterattack. Never do the expected! Bruce Lee called this approach "broken-rhythm fighting;" it features a willingness to break patterns, ideally throwing off the opponent. From my interviews with dozens and dozens of people over the years about violent encounters, I think I can safely make the generalization that violent encounters seldom go as planned. Parties planning violent encounters cannot factor in anything about you, the attendee and star of the event; therefore, flexibility is everything.

This creativity can extend into all different arenas of self-defense, including the location and use of makeshift weapons. On a dayhike a couple of years ago in the Rockies, I passed a group of hikers that set off all kinds of fear alarms inside my head. I had just about reached the turnaround point of this round-trip hike and increased my speed to create distance. As soon as I got out of sight, I picked up two fist-sized rocks, one for each hand, and stuffed the rocks in the pockets of my fleece jacket. When I passed the group on the way back to the trailhead, I wore a grin on my face and kept my hands in my pockets.

"Whatsa'matter?" one said. "Hands cold?"

"You bet!" I said, and kept on grinning and trucking on down the trail. Eventually, I jettisoned my ballast and cruised on home. Other examples of makeshift weapons present in the backcountry include sticks, branches, logs, pinecones, gravel, and just plain dirt.

In a potentially violent encounter, I'll do anything that might give me an edge if the encounter were to proceed. I might limp, leaning on my hiking stick. I might make up a lie ("My dog is a junkie."). I might pretend to be left-handed instead of right-handed. I might palm a canister of pepper spray the moment I go to Condition Red.

If you survive a violent encounter, it will result from your ability to control your fear, to keep your mind functioning, and to take advantage of even the smallest opportunity.

Non-Lethal Weapons

Before we take another step up the self-defense ladder, let's talk in a bit more detail about non-lethal weapons, improvised or otherwise. I generally think that any weapon is better than no weapon at all. Hand-to-hand fighting is a truly frightening concept, especially if you're a woman and your opponent outweighs you by 100 pounds. A rock or a stick or a can of pepper spray can't completely solve your problems, but they can buy you time. If you've got to fight, grab an improvised weapon of some sort, deliver a blow (or a spray) and, as we have said earlier, get the heck out of Dodge!

If you're going to carry a spray of any kind, I suggest you hit the Internet and locate a pepper spray offered on a police supplier site. Sprays purchased over the counter tend to vary in quality and effectiveness. Strangely enough, I've experienced tear gas a lot, during both riot situations and training simulations with the military and the police. Some spray works great; some doesn't work at all. The most effective (and therefore, least enjoyable) spray I have ever experienced was a police pepper spray called Mr. Clear Out, which was hell in a spray can. The spray is absorbed through the skin, especially in areas that are moist and sweaty; my skin crawls just remembering the stuff. I've also been in gas that mostly just made me tear up and get pissed off. Don't assume that a spray will completely disable your assailant, no matter what it says on the label; spray it, then use the seconds it might buy to retreat.

Notice how I keep coming back to retreat here. I'll take the retreat option whenever it appears—as long as it won't put me at greater risk. That caveat is very important. Once a violent encounter is underway, when I assume Condition

Black, my mind-set shifts to neutralizing the threat. But as you employ these principles of non-lethal self-defense, remember that the option to retreat remains ever present. The trail differs from an urban environment, in which it is easy to get cornered. To borrow a phrase from my old pal Rozelle, think "cut and run." If you have to fight, ruthlessly deliver the most telling blows you can. Then bail. Don't ever attack and then step back to admire your handiwork! If you have to attack, attack and move; then attack again. Keep moving. Watch boxers on television—they almost never stand and punch. It's attack and move. Attack and retreat. Move, whenever you can.

13

The Question

Welcome to the Worst Case

WELL, YOU'VE FINALLY COME TO THE PLACE at which you didn't want to arrive. You've tried to avoid, to retreat, to placate, to use all of the non-lethal methods at your disposal; you've come to the end of your rope, and you remain threatened. What is your next step? According to the self-defense strategy, presentation and engagement fill the next two steps on the decision tree. I define "presentation" as the showing of your weapon, whether it is a walking stick or a firearm. When you present your weapon or assume a martial arts fighting stance or raise your fist, you essentially give a final warning, intended to communicate that you are prepared to fight with the weapon at hand. "Engagement," that is, actually defending yourself with your chosen weapon, follows close on the heels of presentation. To be effective in ending a conflict, you must establish just how far you are willing to go and actually proceed to that limit.

The Hard Part

We now encounter the hard part. A few chapters back, we talked about "The Question"—*how far are you willing to go to protect your own life, or the lives of others in your care?* If you choose to use lethal force for self-defense, you must be absolutely sure of your answer. Clarity of your limits is crucial because if you're bluffing, if you haven't truly and honestly answered "The Question," in a real situation your assailant will quite possibly kill you. It is that simple. It doesn't matter if the weapon you choose to use is a gun, a knife, or a rock; you must be prepared to use that weapon to its full capacity. I once met a woman who had been mugged and wanted to buy a gun for protection. I taught her to shoot myself, but the more we talked, the more I realized that she hadn't really thought the whole thing through. Why, she kept asking, can't I bluff or "only shoot him in the leg?"

Let's answer her question in two parts. First of all, I told the woman, you can't bluff because *predators always recognize prey.* Violent criminals are no strangers to violence. Usually, such individuals have had a weapon pointed at them before. The unfolding of violent crime involves each party trying to get into his or her opponent's head. All of the tools that I've tried to impart to you thus far are also available to your assailant. He or she tries to read *you*, to get a sense of what's going on in *your head.* If you prepare to use lethal force, and your assailant senses that you are not serious, you will likely lose the battle. If you have a weapon your assailant will turn it against you. The ultimate escalation, you've now lost your weapon and armed your enemy.

Secondly, you cannot just "shoot him in the leg" because this partial action will not satisfy your objective to stop your assailant. As an analogy, when a small fire burns in your kitchen and you grab your fire extinguisher, what do you hope to accomplish? To put the fire out, right? And you have limited resources with which to accomplish this; fire extinguishers won't keep spraying forever. So to maximize the chances that you will extinguish the fire, you direct your limited fire-fighting resources directly at the center of the fire. You don't spray around the outside edges of the fire to keep it from spreading—it's burning a hole through your kitchen floor, after all. You don't give the right side of the fire a miniscule squirt in the hopes that the fire will quit on its own. You don't do these things to mess around with even a small fire because you understand completely that, unless you act decisively, the fire will destroy your house and maybe even kill you. This is the mind-set we must adopt when we fear for our lives and act on that fear. When I pick up my fire extinguisher, I must have the intent of *stopping* the fire. If I am forced to pick up a weapon, I must have the intent of *stopping* a lethal threat against me or against someone under my responsibility.

A few chapters back, when we first talked about "The Question," we strove to discover how far each of us was willing to go to protect ourselves. In general legal terms, I, as a reasonable person, am legally able to respond with deadly force when I believe that I am in imminent danger of death or serious bodily harm that can only be averted by the use of deadly force against the assailant. In such a case, my sole, singular, and only goal is to *make the assailant stop immediately.* My only concern is ending the lethal threat against me or against those in my care. Immediately. Period.

This goal reiterates what our goal has been throughout this book. Every point in our decision tree has had as its aim ending the threat against us immediately. We plan; we avoid; we retreat; we placate; we try non-lethal means; we do everything we can to end the threat against us immediately.

As perhaps they should be, the issues regarding the use of lethal force are complex and very subjective. What does it mean to be in imminent danger of death or serious bodily harm? What is the gravest extreme? Is it the same for me as it is for you? Of course, the answers to these questions differ from person to person, so I can only offer broad characteristics. As a general rule, as I said above, you are legally justified in using lethal force to protect yourself, or a third party, from imminent death or serious bodily injury. From a legal standpoint, you'll be judged by what is referred to as the "reasonable person" rule—would a reasonable person in your situation fear for his or her life? Every situation is unique, but I can carve out a few factors to assist you in determining what constitutes fear of imminent death or bodily harm. The main question that begs answering is: *Does your assailant have both the opportunity and the ability to inflict serious bodily damage or death upon you?*

In order for you to justify the use of lethal force, the answers to both parts of this question need to be "yes." A guy standing a quarter of a mile away from you on the trail, who shouts, "I'm going to kill you!" isn't in a position to do so. If you are a single woman on the trail faced with two men who approach from 10 feet away, I would argue that both opportunity and ability exist, even if the men are apparently unarmed. A disparity-of-force issue always arises when more than one assailant is involved, particularly when the attackers are men and the potential victim is a woman.

What if you're attacked in your tent at night? In this situation, I would respond immediately with force, up to and including lethal force, because I could only assume that a stealth attacker in the middle of the night meant me serious bodily harm.

Obviously, the sight of any weapon in the hand of an attacker (whether that weapon is a gun, sheath knife, folding knife, or bludgeon of any sort) affects the opportunity/ability decisions. What you personally know also impacts those decisions. For example, you know from reading this book that a person 21 feet away with a knife can deliver a fatal blow in 1.5 seconds. You therefore know that you can't possibly let a person with a knife come any closer than 21 feet. And if your response time to an approaching threat is slower than 1.5 seconds, the maximum distance you must keep between you and the armed person lengthens considerably. Thus, your preparation, physical and mental, also contributes to the equation.

What if someone says they're going to kill you? Well, so what? Do they have the ability to kill you, and do they have the opportunity to kill you? More than one person has suggested that I should die, but I have never responded with deadly force, because the people had neither the ability nor the opportunity to carry out their threats. Every situation is different, and you must evaluate various types of encounters until you feel comfortable that you'll have the ability to make a sound judgment quickly, with the use of tactical information, if such an occasion arose.

A Final Look at Limits

While you consider your limits, I'll tell you a little about mine. When I go into the backcountry, I am prepared to use lethal force if I am faced with a life-threatening situation. My philosophy boils down to a simple statement: When I leave the confines of civilization, I personally accept that the responsibility for my own safety rests solely on me. I talked earlier about how, in cave diving, the "rules of the road" didn't include the buddy system so familiar to recreational scuba divers. As I said, cave divers share the tacit understanding that in the hostile underwater-cave environment, you are on your own. If you suffer a catastrophic malfunction, you have the responsibility for saving yourself.

I'll bet that when you first read this, it bothered you a little. No matter how much we protest otherwise, we are urban creatures. We like the security that comes from being surrounded by lots of people just like us and from knowing that we can usually obtain help quickly in our infrastructure. We like our instant 911 link to emergency personnel, our cellphones, and our overall connectedness. We like the fact that everything follows certain rules, stated and unstated.

We don't want to have the need for a lethal force option, because we strive to believe that all situations can be resolved without resorting to violence. Anyway, someone— the police, a spouse, a friendly stranger, the military, Spiderman—will help us or come to our call in our moment of need. Besides, it won't happen to us, right? Bad things happen to other people. We are safe.

I think that in the final analysis, we are afraid to emulate Dorothy in the *Wizard of Oz* and take a peak behind the Wizard's curtain because we don't want to believe that the violence is *inside* us, not *outside* us. We obtain greater comfort by believing that any weapon we choose to use is a strange talisman with the power to *make* us evil, to *make* us be something that we fundamentally are not. We cling to this belief because if this is untrue, then the capacity for violence, for doing evil, must live inside us. Over the years, I have come to believe in the human capacity to create violence. As a result, I have also come to believe that the responsibility for my own safety rests not with the police, or with the government, or with society at large, but with me. Therefore, if at some point in my travels, I cannot avoid, retreat, placate, or otherwise defuse another person, I will use whatever level of force is necessary.

What You Must Do

If you have now searched your soul and have discovered that your answer to "The Question" is that you will use violent force to protect yourself or people that fall under your responsibility if faced with imminent death or serious bodily harm, you must:

- *Train for the moment.* Know what will work and what won't work for whatever weapons you choose to use. Almost every community has courses on a variety of armed and unarmed self-defense techniques.
- *Learn what you must about the laws of self-defense.* It is imperative that you understand your obligations and responsibilities in order to act legally.
- *Learn from the best.* Top-notch classes in both civilian self-defense and in protecting yourself with a firearm are offered in various organizations. Not only will these classes increase your own confidence level, but they will also help you understand the legal, moral, and ethical dimensions of self-defense.
- *Practice.* No book can train you in self-defense techniques; true training comes from immense practice.

Self-defense techniques involve precise skills, and like any precision skill, they require on-going repetition to retain proficiency.

14

Presentation and Engagement

Lethal Defense

IN BRANCA'S SELF-DEFENSE DECISION TREE, "presentation" comes between the non-lethal and the lethal defense of the victim's life. The victim has done everything he could not to arrive at this junction. He has practiced all the tricks of avoidance; he has retreated or attempted to retreat; he has tried various techniques of placation; he has used whatever non-lethal means he has at his disposal. Presentation means that if the victim has a gun or any other weapon, he draws it. "Engagement" is the use of that weapon.

Usually, the situation quickly reaches resolution at the presentation stage. A weapon changes the balance. Think about the words of a woman that I interviewed years ago. An emergency room nurse and a very committed, very caring person, the woman got off the late shift one night and was grabbed by a rapist on the way to her car. The man dragged her into the bushes and smacked her around. While he fumbled to get out of his pants, she drew a legal gun from her purse and proceeded to engage him with the weapon.

His last words were "Hey that's not fair!"

Interestingly enough, the vast, vast majority of all assaults end with the presentation of a firearm; the numbers are as high as 97% from some experts. This constitutes the central breaking point between gun and antigun people. If the assault is ended before it starts, no record of a crime being committed exists. Gun opponents say that a gun is more dangerous to its owner; gun proponents say that the statistics overlook the number of assaults prevented at the presentation stage. We will be spending the next chapter looking at the firearm option and considering whether or not it is right for you and your lifestyle. Carrying a gun is an extremely serious matter, and demands some attention; we will offer it that attention shortly.

The Surprise Attack

I suspect that a question lurks in the back of your head, and it's now time to bring that question to the forefront. Let's return to the wilderness, maybe to one of the mosquito-ridden trails on the edges of the Everglades in Florida over-hung with Spanish moss. Suppose you are serenely hiking along when you turn a corner and run into a couple of guys, one of who points a gun at you and commands, "Hand me your pack." In such a situation, despite your best efforts, you find yourself between the proverbial rock and a hard place. And in such a situation, your course of action is summed up in a word much like "avoidance" with regard to its negative connotations—you will submit.

Go With the Odds

I would submit when I knew I couldn't win. If an assailant points a gun at my face and yells, "Give it up," I'll give it up, even if I am also armed with a gun. I once asked Dane Burns, a former mountain guide, a self-defense trainer, and one of the most thoughtful people I know on these issues when he would submit. He said this: "The reality is that in an armed situation, most people don't get hurt." That means that most people submit and, in so doing, survive—therefore, go with the odds. If my intuition tells me that what I am facing is a shakedown, I'll be more than happy to hand over my wallet. I can always get more stuff. I can't get more life. Nothing you own is worth risking your life for. I had a friend, a superb athlete, who spent his last few painful years in a wheelchair. He had gotten "pissed off" during a mugging in Washington D.C. He'd already turned over his wallet to his assailant, and the mugger was actually running away when my friend decided to chase him down and "teach him a lesson." The mugger turned and shot my friend.

Fighting Back

Ideally, thanks to your heightened awareness and honed intuition, you're not going to find yourself in the surprise attack situation. However, everybody gets surprised and, just like anything else, you must prepare yourself for this eventuality.

Due to the odds of submission, assailants hardly ever expect their victims to fight back. They almost invariably assume that their victims will submit, and that is generally what victims do. You can use this expectation to bend the scales in your favor. As a quick example, assume you sleep

deeply in your tent when you're awakened by the sound of
somebody slitting open the fabric of your tent and stepping
inside. You, of course, lay in a sleeping bag with the zippers
up, effectively already bagged. Your course of action: Unbag
yourself and attack with whatever you can lay your hands
on. Remember *aggressiveness* from the previous chapter?
Use it. Remember *ruthlessness?* Here's where you spool it
out. Do not talk (although, if you're in a campground with
other people, a scream is appropriate); do not placate; do
nothing but attack with every fiber of your being. Nothing is
quite so disconcerting to an assailant than a sudden, vicious
attack in the dark. You need to consider and plan for such
an attack precisely because it's so difficult. I have actually
thought about how such an attack would go and have outlined a strategy. And because it is so awkward, your response
needs to be as rapid and violent as possible.

While we're on the subject of camping, I'll take this
opportunity to present my Safety Rules for Campsites.
While the bulk of this book assumes you'll be actually in
transit to someplace when and if you have an unpleasant
encounter, you also need to be aware when you set up
camp.

SAFETY RULES FOR CAMPSITES

1. *Make sure that when you think you're in the middle of
   nowhere, you actually are in the middle of nowhere.* A
   particularly horrific backcountry double murder in 1996
   transpired at a campsite that appeared to sit in a location
   remote from the trail, but actually lay only 155 feet from
   a heavily traveled highway teeming with predators. You
   bought all those maps for your trip; look at them. Make
   sure your pristine wilderness campsite isn't a hop, skip,

and a jump from an interstate rest area (which, when I lived in Florida, the natives referred to as "killing grounds").

2. *When in doubt, herds are better.* If you're traveling alone and you've gotten a "ding," consider selecting a campsite where one or two other campers have set up their tents. If you've experienced a serious "ding," I'd mention it to the other campers—"Would you mind if I camped here tonight? I passed some really strange people a few miles back . . . "

3. *Camp unobtrusively.* All of us have seen campers who, for some strange reason, camp astride the trail. Instead of adopting this approach, make your ideal campsite one that goes virtually unnoticed by people traveling by. Camping in this manner carries out one of my own and my partner's Third World Rules—*draw no attention*. It also makes you a more considerate camper.

4. *Camp efficiently.* Become proficient at setting and breaking camp. Maintaining a few camps in below-zero weather will swiftly teach you all the efficiency you will ever need. Efficient camping will also assist you in projecting a confident, competent attitude.

5. *Sleep lightly.* A SWAT cop once asked for my advice in solving an interesting problem—she'd missed a call-out because she had slept through both her beeper and a telephone call. I suggested that sleep, like most of our other functions, could be programmed to some degree. Instead of constantly thinking of herself as a deep sleeper, I recommended that she start mentally telling herself that she always woke up for the phone and always woke up for her beeper. It worked for her, just as in Farley Mowat's classic book, *Never Cry Wolf,* about his time in the

Canadian North, Mowat taught himself to sleep like a wolf. Wolves catnap and can then come fully awake at the drop of a pin. Then they return to napping.

When You Don't Have Moves

I'm not going to lie to you. When a gun has been thrust in your face, you probably don't have a move on the board. Some martial arts and self-defense schools teach *disarms*, that is, methods for taking the gun away from the assailant. A few years back, when my old martial arts school was teaching disarms, I brought an empty gun to class, and we worked through the techniques. Much to everyone's surprise, no one was able to take the gun away from me before I could get off a shot.

Most of the non-police disarm techniques that I have seen assume that the assailant is either distracted or is in some way uncomfortable with the gun. That is one heck of an assumption. I have seen disarms that work taught by crack police instructors. In every case, the techniques require split-second timing and a working knowledge of guns. These techniques also require endless repetition to master. The one that I do know fairly well, I would only consider using if I felt that my death was imminent, that I had truly run out of options.

If you have to submit, don't stop thinking. Look for avenues of retreat opening up, for people coming down the trail, and for any other incoming tactical information that may change your situation. You must remain aware and take advantage of any opportunity that presents itself to you.

Looking for Armed Assailants

Potentially lethal situations can be avoided in many cases by knowing what to look for in terms of whether or not your trail-mates may be armed hooligans in disguise. Therefore, I make it a point to examine people I meet on the trail to see whether they might have a weapon. Interestingly enough, most people who carry a gun tend to telegraph that fact, if you know what to look for. Novelist Jerry Ahern became not only an expert on concealed weapons, but also a skilled holster designer after he and his wife, Sharon, spent about a dozen years writing a wildly successful men's adventure series. He combined his skills to sum up that information in his book *CCW: Carrying Concealed Weapons*. In this book, Ahern includes a quite succinct description of what to look for when determining whether or not a person is armed: "Is there something out of synch about a person, perhaps in attire or body movement? . . . Look for bumps, bulges, outlines and unnatural actions." Things that might indicate this incongruity include:

- Fanny pack worn in the front of the body or slightly to one side (usually the left, to facilitate a right-hand draw).
- An additional small bag (approximately 6"×9") worn on the waist-belt of the pack.
- Anything sagging—guns are relatively heavy items, and a person unfamiliar with carrying one spends a lot of time tugging.

I am also watchful of sheath knives (although I assume that you, like me, never go into the woods without some type of a knife). The bigger the sheath knife, the more wary I tend to be of the person wearing it. I have seen hunting guides in Alaska who never carry anything larger than a 4-inch skinning blade. If someone on the trail actually carries a blade that looks like it escaped from a Sylvester Stallone movie, I give it a "ding."

In the next chapter we'll discuss the increasing abundance of handguns in the outdoors and how this affects you as a backcountry enthusiast. We touched on this controversial issue slightly in this chapter when we discussed the defense of your life against assailants who threaten you with guns. As part of your self-defense strategy, you may decide to pick a weapon with which to present and engage; that weapon may be a gun. Many, many considerations and responsibilities come along with the ownership of a gun, and these must be dealt with on moral, social, ethical, and legal levels. I will attempt to present the information about guns with which I am familiar in a very objective manner and encourage you to do more extensive research on your own. After all, it is you who must make the choice.

15

Handgun Use in the Outdoors

The Firearms Option

NOTHING PERSONIFIES LETHAL FORCE more than handguns. More and more people currently carry handguns on their travels in the outdoors or otherwise than ever before. This trend leads to immense social debate and to a myriad of questions: How can you protect yourself against those with guns? Should you personally carry a gun? If so, what factors are important in terms of equipment, training, and the various responsibilities you undertake if you become a gun owner? If you do choose to carry a handgun, you must respect the many laws and obligations that surround carrying a handgun. I would not necessarily advocate that you carry a gun. I do; however, if you do decide to carry a gun, you must be absolutely cognizant of your responsibilities.

A gun is not a magic wand that repels bad guys. Think of it instead as one possible tool in your self-defense strategy, like the fire extinguisher we talked about earlier. If you strive to prevent fires in your home, a fire extinguisher would not be your first purchase. Instead, you would analyze your home with an eye toward minimizing fire risks. Does old wiring spark every time you turn on a light switch? Are fire-escape routes mapped out and communicated to members of the household? Has everyone been educated on the safe operation of electric appliances, matches, candles, and fireplaces? If not, the solutions for minimizing risks include new wiring, clear options for retreat, and safety training; the fire extinguisher provides solely secondary protection. In the same way, a handgun will only provide secondary protection, and requires an astounding amount of training to operate safely and accurately—much more than a fire extinguisher would demand. Before you make the decision to purchase a gun, you need to study your lifestyle, your home, your family, and the backcountry activities you do. Make sure that you have fixed the wiring, established options for retreat, and trained for self-defense. Only after you establish this foundation should you even consider the use of a handgun.

Those people who have owned and used guns for years have quite literally changed their lifestyles to accommodate that decision. Houses must be secure. Locks must be strong. Excellent gun safes must be invested in. The fact that a person owns and carries guns should not be broadcast. The actual gun forms one small part of a firearm self-defense system. Other contributing ingredients include the gun's ammunition, a way to reload the gun, a way to carry the gun, a place to store the gun and, most importantly, *training* on how to use the gun and on the legal obligations of gun owners. Gun control and licensing, another area with which you must become familiar if you decide to go down this path, involves many facets as well.

Gun Control and Licensing

Despite what you may have read or heard, gun ownership is strictly controlled in most areas. In some cities, such as Chicago and New York, you cannot legally own a handgun at all. At the very least, in every state potential gun owners have to go through a federal (and probably a state) background check. Also, various fees are charged for the appropriate licensure of a gun.

Once a gun is owned, actually carrying a gun also brings with it certain legal requirements. Counties, states, and municipalities closely and fervently control who conceals and carries guns, and how they do so. To legally carry a gun, one needs a concealed carry permit, the obtaining of which can be a surprisingly complex process. In some jurisdictions, such a permit may be impossible to secure. The concealed carry permit applications can result in police files three-quarters of an inch thick; police files on repeat felons are thinner.

Concerns about concealed carry permits extend to the backcountry as well. If you're on the trail for any length of time, you are likely to move through several legal jurisdictions. Every one of these jurisdictions probably has different laws regarding concealed weapons. For example, trails in or through national parks do not allow firearms at all. It's the gun owner's responsibility to know all this; ignorance of the law is neither an excuse nor a defense.

Household Agreement on a Firearm Strategy

Before one chooses the firearms option, other aspects to consider crop up. First and foremost, every potential gun owner must discuss the firearms option with his or her family and come to an agreement on strategy. If a gun is going to be kept in the house, every adult residing in the house should be familiar with loading, unloading, making safe, and shooting the gun. I believe that goes for older teenagers as well. Younger children must also learn about gun safety so as to prevent accidental shootings—the NRA's "Eddie Eagle" program provides some of the best training for this purpose.

If any disagreement regarding whether or not to keep a gun in the house cannot be resolved, the firearm option must be discarded as a possibility. As an illustration, a family of three once asked me for an opinion on their gun strategy. The father kept a loaded, WWII bolt-action rifle under his bed for protection. His wife was "physically sickened" by the gun and pretended that it simply wasn't there. She informed me that she had once "screamed bloody murder" at her 17-year-old son (an honor student and, by all accounts, an exceptional kid) when he asked to see the rifle. My opinion was that this particular household was a disaster-in-waiting on more counts than I could tick off on both hands. I urged the family to get rid of the gun immediately. The mother's mega-strong antigun response negated the chance of both class training and private training (a suggestion that I made early on in my discussions with the family). Also, her refusal to allow her mature son any access to the gun increased the risk, as he could not obtain knowledge of either the mechanical workings or of the safety aspects of the gun. If a gun owner keeps a gun in the house, and is in a relationship or has a family, there must be some kind of consensus on self-defense strategy among family members, or disaster will strike. It comes down to communication. Everyone in the household (or on the trail, for that matter) must understand exactly what the self-defense strategy involves and the role they play in that strategy.

Storage Arrangements

As mentioned above, the purchase of a gun, ammunition, and additional loading devices does not a competent gun owner make. Among the systems components that also must be considered are the storage arrangements for the gun and for the associated equipment. Owning and carrying a gun is a staggering responsibility. Every gun owner is ethically, morally, and legally responsible for that gun 24 hours a day, seven days a week. This means that the gun must be either in his or her hand, on his or her person, or otherwise secured every minute of every day. The gun owner must know—not think, not assume, not guess—absolutely that the gun is either in his or her hand, on his or her person, or otherwise secured. He or she cannot delegate this responsibility; he or she does not get a day off.

And by "secured," I mean locked away. A gun safe provides the optimal level of security, and gun safes come in sizes from small single-gun safes to fairly substantial multi-gun safes. Some single-gun safes are designed to be opened quickly, using a finger-keyed combination. The next best security option is a locking cabinet designed to hold guns. The third best alternative is a fireproof safe. None of these options come cheap. In fact, if you choose the firearms option, you will buy into an expensive proposition.

Safety First, Last, and Always

Guns are like gravity—they work all the time. If you drop your PowerBar, you expect it to fall to the ground, because gravity never sleeps. In a similar manner, those who choose to own and carry guns give up all excuses, morally, ethically, and legally. Where the bullet goes and what the bullet does become the sole and exclusive responsibility of the gun owner, legally, ethically, and morally. He or she will answer for every bullet fired in defense in a court of law, and he or she will answer for every bullet fired in his or her heart and mind for the rest of his or her life.

Given that about 50 percent of all the households in America own at least one gun, amazingly few gun accidents actually occur. I would wager a bet that every one of those accidents results from breaking one of the following four rules. It's no different from cave diving. There aren't many rules, but the consequences of breaking one is dire. Given that, the four simple gun-handling safety rules are:

1. *All guns are always loaded.* The first thing I do when I touch a gun is to check to see if it's loaded. If it's loaded, I empty it. If I set it down on a table and pick it back up, I check it again. If I have it in my hand for longer than a few minutes, I check it again, just in case a cartridge sneaked in. This needs to be an unconscious reflex... touch a gun, clear it.

2. *Do not touch the trigger until you are ready for the gun to fire.* Guns won't fire unless you make them fire. The way you make them fire is by pulling the trigger. There is no such thing as an accidental discharge. They only go off when you pull the trigger. If you don't pull the trigger, it won't fire. Protecting yourself with a firearm requires a conscious act of will—aim and fire.

3. *Be absolutely sure of your target.* The absolute basis of current firearms training involves establishing a certainty of the target. Remember that the world we live in is three-dimensional—things sit behind the intended target,

in front of the intended target, and beside the intended target. No matter how much chemistry is dumped into your bloodstream, no matter how loudly the alarms go off in your head, no matter what, you must be sure of the target. Say that a gun owner has set up for camp late one night, and a speed hiker comes barreling into the dark shelter without warning. If that gun owner has any doubts about his or her ability to correctly identify that this speed hiker should not be a target of gunfire, that gun owner should not bring the gun on such an excursion or carry it at any time. This possibility is a common concern as the number of hikers carrying guns increases. Presenting the weapon at the right time, when escalation of force has gone as high as it can go, is a learned skill, for which you must obtain formal training.

4. *Do not point the gun at anything you are not willing to see destroyed, including yourself.* This rule is an article of religious faith with me. A gun owner should never point a gun at anyone or anything he or she doesn't want to see destroyed, blown to bits, or killed; nor should he or she allow anyone else to do so in his or her presence. I have physically taken a gun away from at least one relatively famous pop star and I have also risked the serious ire of police officers on the range who weren't careful enough. Just like the rules of cave diving, the four rules of gun handling are written in stone, are not negotiable, and are absolute. Those rules will keep everyone safe if they are followed to the letter.

What You Must Do

In Chapter 13, we talked about what you must do if you choose to use a lethal self-defense option if an assailant threatens your life or the life of someone in your care. We must expand this list if a firearms option is chosen as follows:

- *Engage in safety training.* Learn how the gun works and how it doesn't work. You can obtain information about safety classes from most locations where guns can be purchased.
- *Educate yourself in the laws of self-defense.* Most states that have provisions for concealed carry permits also have a requirement for training in the laws of that state, so classes are usually available and not difficult to locate. You can also ask attorneys for an interpretation of the self-defense laws of the state in which you live.
- *Learn to shoot.* Remember that shooting a handgun is much harder than it appears to be on television. Like any precision skill, shooting requires ongoing practice to retain proficiency. Go to the shooting range and maintain your target practice. If you're so inclined, get involved in practical shooting competition, as this environment will demand both skill and speed in tense situations; these traits closely resemble those characteristics you're likely to find in violent encounters.
- *Learn from the best.* Top-notch classes in both civilian self-defense and in protecting yourself with a firearm are offered throughout the country. If you do decide to carry a gun, I unconditionally suggest that you take one or more of these classes. Not only will it increase your own confidence level, but it will also help you understand the legal, moral, and ethical dimensions of self-defense as a whole.

16

An End and a Beginning

AFTER ALL THIS TALK about violent encounters, lethal force, and weapons of various descriptions, you're probably fairly wound up. Some stray, baby bits of adrenaline may even course through your veins just from imagining the types of situations we've discussed, and you may be feeling more panicked than ever about the potential crimes that may await you in the backcountry. Now, like a cool-down at the end of an intense workout or a meditative stance you might adopt at the end of long hike, let's take a moment to reflect on where we've been and where we are now.

I think it's safe to say that *Trail Safe* has forced us to walk some trails we didn't want to walk. Now that we've passed over that ground, can we now answer the question of how to keep ourselves safe? Can we banish any irrational fears about the outdoors that may have crept into our lives and feel confident that we have prepared ourselves for battling those risks that are under our control? I hope so.

Trail Safe began by introducing the concepts of intuition, awareness, and fear, and demonstrating how paying attention to and utilizing these tools can provide us with a powerful self-defense mechanism. Then I told you about two practical steps that should be taken in preparation for any trip: the completion of a risk assessment and fleshing that assessment out with some detailed, specific planning for your trip. Finally, we explored the various options available to you if you have the bad luck to actually face a potentially violent assailant, all the way from avoiding that situation, right up to engaging a weapon with an aim to end the threat against you. I asked you some important questions about your own personal definitions of limits when it comes to lethal force, which I hope you have considered seriously. I also discussed the training and responsibilities that go along with selecting a lethal-force option, especially as those relate to the use of handguns in the outdoors or elsewhere.

At the beginning of *Trail Safe*, we discussed the perceived risk of going into the backcountry and encountering violent crime, versus the actual risk of being threatened while on such excursions. I said that there is a perception that crime is increasing on our mountain trails, around our glacier lakes, and at our trailheads and campgrounds. But I also said that this perception is just that: a perception. In reality, violent crime has been steadily decreasing for years. Despite the recent high-profile school shootings, public schools are actually safer than they have ever been. Violence in the workplace has been also steadily decreasing throughout the end of the 1990s. In fact, despite what you may have seen last night on the evening news, the simple truth is that unless you have chosen to involve yourself in the drug culture, you suffer from substance abuse problems, or you are actively involved in some other illegal activity, you will probably go through your entire life without becoming a victim of violence. Throughout *Trail Safe* I haven't played the "statistics game." But regardless of the scary stories that you may have read in the paper or heard about on television, being alone on any trail is still far safer than partying in Times Square on New Year's Eve.

But that doesn't absolve us of the responsibility of being aware. In the end, whether we are two days out in the Alaska Range or sitting at home in our recliner with the remote, we hold the ultimate responsibility for our own well-being. This responsibility is inherent in the human condition; it cannot be assigned to another person, to an agency, or even to a police department.

A mental freedom comes from the knowledge that you have the tools and abilities to take care of yourself; that regardless of how far you are from the resources at 911, you can move smoothly and comfortably through the world. More importantly, clear benefits come from living in Condition Green and from maintaining a relaxed awareness of the world around us. We see more; we're able to notice the beauty of the trails around us, the comings and goings of the wild creatures, and the subtle changes wrought by the shifting seasons. By being aware, we are able to become more than a simple tourist; rather, we can become one with our environment, as nature intended.

Years ago, I got some advice from one of my first martial arts instructors from Korea, whose command of English doesn't rival his mastery of the Korean arts. He explained to me, as best he could, what my problem as a beginner martial artist was. Like many Westerners, he said, I saw martial arts as a *thing*, as something in a box like a bicycle or a pair of

Nikes. And I kept this box outside of my house. That, he said with finality, was my problem: "box outside of house."

Translated, this means that I did indeed see martial arts as a thing, a skill to simply be learned and used, the way one might learn to ride a bicycle and use it to ride to work. Instead, I needed to understand that martial arts is a world view, a way of relating to the sticks and rocks and people around me. As my instructor told me, "The box is house."

It has been a long time since I stepped into the circle to fight; I no longer honestly think of myself as a martial artist as the term is defined. I do, however, think a lot about the "box as the house," and about how we as human beings relate to the world. The ideas presented in *Trail Safe* need to be treated in the same way. In order to really utilize these tools, they must become part of your world view, part of your "house." These strategies are the bedrocks to my own relationship with the world. They enable me to enjoy my surroundings intelligently and to "live in the moment" to the best of my abilities.

I have over the years spent a large amount of time with consultants, with speakers, with trainers, with business executives; I have heard the words "live in the moment" repeated endlessly as a secret for business and for personal success. I've heard a lot fewer words on how that actually works. How do we "live in the moment?" Does it take a weekend seminar? A lifetime of study? A 12-cassette course to listen to in the car? A life-threatening experience? I think that we "live in the moment" by programming ourselves to live strategically, to adjust those software systems we are born with to allow us to move through the natural world as a fish moves through water, or the way a bird moves through the air. I've watched my pals the parrots move not only through the air, but also through the tides of emotions that mark their world, just as emotions mark our lives. The ranges of emotions are not particularly different from the various intensities of wind and water: breezes become hurricanes; trickles become floods. Ultimately, it isn't our emotions that are the turning points in our lives, just as it is not the hurricane or the flood. Rather, it is our reaction, our response, to those things that define both who we are and how we will live.

Predators will always circle their prey, and that is neither good nor bad, but is simply the nature of things. Through our senses, though our awareness, through our intuitive skills, through our brains, we have the ability to walk safely through the dark woods and see, not the Big Bad Wolf, but the wonders of nature that await us there.

Publisher's Note

The staff and management of Wilderness Press do not believe that the spread of guns throughout our preserved wild places will render anyone safer. Even taking a weapon into the outdoors can change philosophically how we regard natural places. We, at Wilderness Press, feel that perceptions and concerns about personal safety in the wilderness are real, and that books such as Michael Bane's *Trail Safe* go a long way toward addressing what you can do to feel safer and prevent mishaps. Beyond that, we ask you to carefully consider options other than lethal force—a resort with pitfalls and serious ramifications for our society. We value Mr. Bane's effort to present many of the issues, and expect that this book may help open a needed dialogue.

Note from The Appalachian Trail Conference

Carrying firearms is illegal on more than 40 percent of the Appalachian Trail and is subject to state laws on the rest of the Trail (primarily National Forests and state gamelands). The Appalachian Trail Conference (ATC) strongly discourages carrying firearms anywhere along the Trail because they change the dynamics of the hiking experience for everyone and because of the risks of accidental shootings, among other reasons. However, ATC is not blind to the fact that some hikers do carry, or are considering carrying, handguns on this and other trails and believes the issues addressed in *Trail Safe* should be considered and debated by all lovers of the outdoors.

Bibliography

Ahern, Jerry. 1996. *CCW: Carrying Concealed Weapons: How to Carry Concealed Weapons and Know When Others Are.* Blacksmith Corporation, Chino Valley, Arizona.

Ayoob, Massad F. 1980. *In the Gravest Extreme.* Police Bookshelf, Concord, New Hampshire.

Bane, Michael. 1998. *Driving on the Edge.* The Lyons Press, New York, New York.

Bane, Michael. 2000. *Over the Edge: A Regular Guy's Odyssey in Extreme Sports.* Wilderness Press, Berkeley, California.

Branca, Andrew F. 1998. *The Law of Self-Defense.* Operon Security, Ltd., Acton, Massachusetts.

Cooper, Jeff. 1972. *Principles of Personal Defense.* Paladin Press, Boulder, Colorado.

de Becker, Gavin. 1997. *The Gift of Fear.* Little, Brown and Company, New York, New York.

Enos, Brian. 1990. *Practical Shooting: Beyond Fundamentals.* Zediker Publishing, Clifton, Colorado.

Glassner, Barry. 1999. *The Culture of Fear.* Basic Books, New York, New York.

Herbert, Frank. 1999. *Dune.* Ace Books, New York, New York.

Lee, Bruce, 1975. *Tao of Jeet Kune Do.* Ohara Publications, Inc., Burbank, California.

Leonard, George, 1992. *Mastery: The Keys to Success and Long-Term Fulfillment.* Plume, New York, New York.

Lott, John R., Jr. 1998. *More Guns: Less Crime*. The University of Chicago Press, Chicago, Illinois, and London, England.

Mowat, Farley. 1983. *Never Cry Wolf*. Bantam, New York, New York.

Musashi, Miyamoto. 1992. *The Book of Five Rings*. Bantam, New York, New York.

Rauch, Walt. 1998. *Real World Survival: What Has Worked For Me*. Rauch & Company, Ltd., Lafayette Hill, Pennsylvania.

Ross, John F. 1999. *The Polar Bear Strategy*. Perseus Books, New York, New York.

Tzu, Sun. 1983. *The Art of War*. Edited and with a Foreword by James Clavell. Delta/Dell, New York, New York.

Index

If you enjoyed *Trail Safe*, by Michael Bane, pick up another of Mr. Bane's books published by Wilderness Press:

Over the Edge: A Regular Guy's Odyseey in Extreme Sports

Wilderness Press invites you to enjoy this except of *Over the Edge*.

To The Edge

IT IS 10 DEGREES BELOW ZERO OUTSIDE MY TENT, and it has been snowing steadily for three days. I keep trying to think of new, inventive ways of keeping warm, but, ultimately, they all boil down to just one—stay in my purple sleeping bag as long as I can, try to will my mind to blankness.

The wind roars, and the tent pops like a piece of rawhide on the end of Indiana Jones' bullwhip.

It is, I think, Indiana Jones who has gotten me into this. At least, he's got to be partially responsible. Him and his keyword, "adventure."

In a few minutes, I will have to crawl out of my marginally warm sleeping bag, punch a hole up, through the snow, crawl out and start digging my out my tent. Welcome to Denali, Mt. McKinley, Alaska, Land of Adventure. I have come to this undefrosted refrigerator of a land to check an item off a list. No, make that, The List. Thirteen items, activities, events that have come to define the outer limits of my life; heck, the outer limits of any life.

It is an over the edge list, a collection of events that nightmares are made of:

Trapped in underwater caves . . .
Trapped on a frozen waterfall . . .

Trapped in Death Valley . . .

Trapped in Alcatraz . . .

And now, trapped on the highest mountain in North America, pinned in by a brutal blizzard and temperatures almost beyond comprehension.

"Wind chill? How about *real damn* cold?"

I twist into as much of a ball as you can twist into in a mummy sleeping bag, avoiding the inevitable.

I am not supposed to be here . . .

I am in my 40s, well past the derring-do years. I am a couch potato; well, maybe I *was* a couch potato. But I know, emphatically, I am not supposed to die in a blizzard on this mountain.

Or am I?

* * * * * *

I first created the list with some friends over pizza and beer after a particularly knarly day of windsurfing in Florida. The next morning, on the desk in my office, lay a cocktail napkin with 13 items scrawled across it.

I though to myself, suppose I really did the list? No, The List, upper case. Suppose I really did it? How crazy is this stuff, anyway? Who are the people who think these things are *fun?*

I mean, it's easy to understand why a person might want to run three miles; harder to understand what drives a person to train to run almost 150 miles across one of the most godforsaken spots in the world, where the asphalt, I will learn, is hot enough to cause the air pockets in the runners' sneakers to explode and the final 13 miles of climbing will bring them from scorching heat to cold approaching freezing.

It's easy to understand the urge to swim a couple of times a week for fitness at the local "Y"; harder to grasp the dark appeal of the Alcatraz swim, the bitter cold waters sluicing in and out of San Francisco Bay, the fog and swirling currents, the real or imagined torpedo-like shapes patrolling the deep channels.

So I come to the risk sports looking, I think, for Indiana Jones. Or, at least, someone like him. Some part and parcel of our mythology, cowboy or samurai, riding the edge jaggies for all they're worth.

Instead, I will find a group of puzzled people with a tiger by the tail, interested not so much in mythology as in touching and holding an experience as ephemeral as spider silk, ghostly as morning mist over a Montana river, an experience made of equal parts of muscle, adrenaline, and a mind that echoes a sneaker commercial . . . just do it . . . do it . . . do it. An experience I touched, however briefly, on a piece of fiberglass in a windy yacht basin.

"I think I know where you're going," one of my many instructors will tell me as we hike along the frozen waterfalls of New Hampshire's Frankenstein Cliffs, named not for Mary Shelley's monster, but for an artist. The temperature will be below zero, and the winds from the valley below will scour the ice, turning it as brittle and fragile as an old window pane. "But how do you plan on getting back?"

But that is still a ways in the future; out of sight; out of reach.

I stare at my cocktail napkin.

Why not? How hard can it be?

I spend an afternoon at the library, looking up events. There is precious little hard information. I can turn on the television and see all manner of this stuff, but hard information is lacking. The more I search, the more extreme sports seems to be terra incognito, the place on the map where there's nothing but a hand-drawn dragon. There are secrets here, I think, a world over the edge of the map. Secrets...

I go back to my office and stare at my cocktail napkin:
1. *Windsurf Big Air*
2. *Kamikaze Downhill*
3. *Escape From Alcatraz*
4. *Whitewater off a Waterfall*
5. *Rock Climb*
6. *Cave Dive*
7. *Ice Climb*
8. *Skydive; whatever those parachute thingies are.*
9. *Skate Marathon*
10. *Dive Really Deep.*
11. *Badwater Death Valley Run*
12. *Iditarod Bike Race*
13. *Denali*

I need a plan. At first, the plan seems easy—I'll scrape up what money I have, go out to Death Valley and tag onto that nightmarish run. Then I'll head on up north to do the Kamikaze Downhill. I'll learn to rock climb, then mountain climb and get certified to SCUBA dive while I'm at it. I'll even learn to swim, something I've been avoiding. The wind howls, and nothing seems impossible. I drive home, clean my equipment, take a handful of aspirin, shower, and bandage my hands. Then I get the morning paper and turn to the classifieds—I'm going to need a mountain bike, I think...